STRENGTH

AND

HOW TO OBTAIN IT,

BY

EUGEN SANDOW,

WITH

ANATOMICAL CHART,

ILLUSTRATING

EXERCISES FOR PHYSICAL DEVELOPMENT.

———

REVISED EDITION.

———

ILLUSTRATED WITH FULL PAGE PORTRAITS OF THE AUTHOR
AND SOME OF HIS PUPILS.

*Reproduced from Photographs by Falk of New York, and
Warwick Brookes of Manchester.*

———

London:

GALE & POLDEN, Ltd.,

2, AMEN CORNER, PATERNOSTER ROW, E.C., AND WELLINGTON WORKS
ALDERSHOT.

———

TWO-AND-SIX NETT

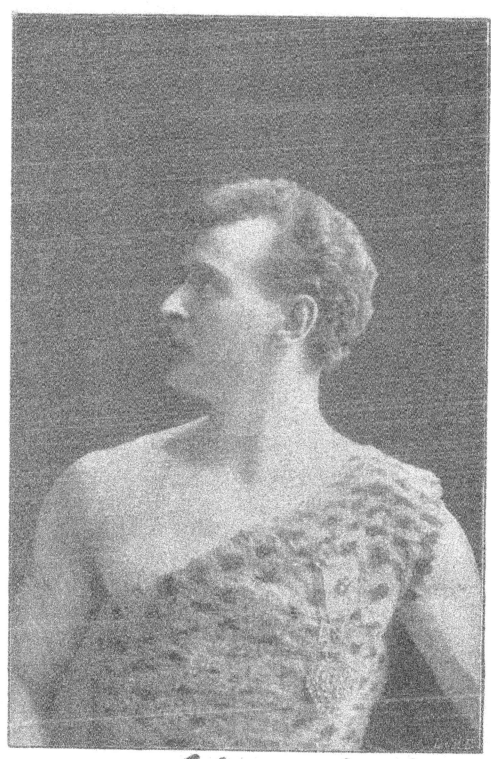

Yours truly
Eugene Ch... ...

PRINTED BY GALE & POLDEN, LTD.,
WELLINGTON WORKS,
ALDERSHOT.

P 328.

CONTENTS.

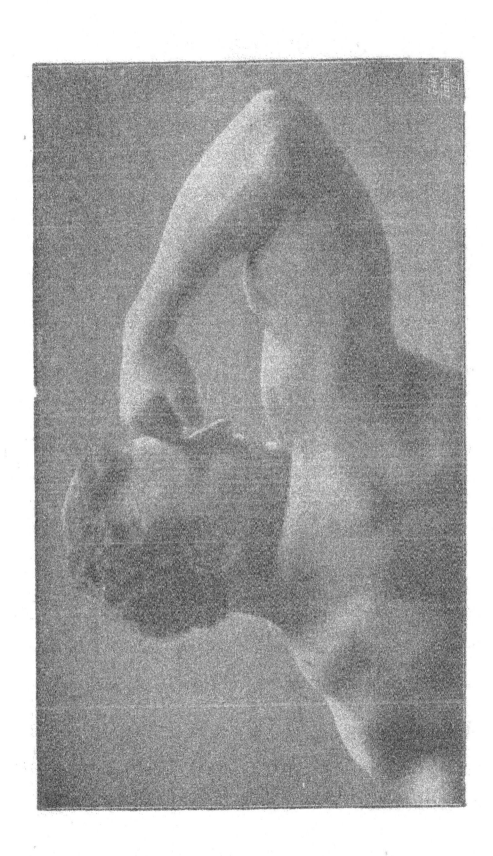

INTRODUCTION.

In writing this book I have taken it as a commonplace that everyone—man, woman, and child—wants to be strong. Without strength—and by strength I mean health, vitality, and a general sense of physical well-being—life is but a gloomy business. Wealth, talent, ambition, the love and affection of friends, the pleasure derived from doing good to those about one, all these things may afford some consolation for being deprived of life's chief blessing, but they can never make up for it. "But," I am constantly being asked, "it is all very well for you to say this, and everyone of sense agrees with you; the point is, can we obtain this much-prized blessing?" In the vast majority of cases I can say unhesitatingly "Yes." You can all be strong, all enjoy the heritage which was intended for you. Not all to the same extent, perhaps. Those who are afflicted with some hereditary disease, who may have unsound organs handed down to them, cannot reasonably expect to get such results as their more fortunate brethren. Still, even they need not despair; even if their condition be such as to put out of the question any such thing as athletics, they can, at all events, attain to such a condition as will permit of their enjoying life, and render them fit to carry on their work without difficulty. And after all, those who wish to be strong for this reason are innumerable. It is only the young and vigorous who desire to excel in athletic pastimes, but the middle-aged and elderly, the delicate women and young children, who yearn for health are countless. I claim that by carefully following out my system, as set out in the following pages, and fully illustrated in the Anatomical Chart at the end of the volume, these results may be attained.

NOTE TO THE SECOND EDITION.

IT is nearly two years since the first edition of "Strength and How to Obtain it" was published, and its success has been very gratifying to me. It plainly demonstrates that the people of my adopted country are gradually beginning to understand and appreciate what is meant by "physical culture," and that my ideas are steadily taking root in productive ground. I am, therefore, encouraged to bring out a new edition of the book, which, I trust, will be an improvement upon its predecessor. Several chapters have been added and a few inaccuracies and ambiguities remedied, and I trust the book in its new form will find favour with my readers. I wish to draw particular attention to chapters V. and VIII., in which I refer to "My 'Grip' Dumb-bell" and to "Physical Culture for Women." There are various other additions to which I need not refer here. Sufficient to say that during the past eighteen months I have learned much, and that so far as lies in my power I have endeavoured to give the benefit of such knowledge as I have acquired to all who believe with me that the cultivation of the body is a sacred and imperative duty.

EUGEN SANDOW.

PART I.

MY SYSTEM OF PHYSICAL CULTURE.

STRENGTH

AND

HOW TO OBTAIN IT.

————➤·◄————

CHAPTER I.

CONCERNING PHYSICAL CULTURE.

It is curious to me to look back a year or two and to
reflect upon the change in public opinion upon this subject which has taken place in so short a time. When I
first began to preach the "gospel of health and
strength" the general tendency was to make fun of me.
Some people called me a fool; others, a charlatan.
Very few indeed took the trouble to see whether there
was anything in my theories, and to test for themselves
their truth or falsity. That was, so to speak, only
yesterday; what an alteration, and an alteration for the
better, is to be observed to-day. I shall not be accused of
undue egotism if I say that my ideas have "caught on."
All over the country, among the young, "physical
culture" is now the rage, and that it is no mere passing
fancy is proved by the fact that those who are no longer
in their first youth are its equally devoted, though
possibly less feverish, disciples.

"And what is physical culture?" is naturally the
question which arises to the lips of those to whom the
subject is still unfamiliar. Let me begin by saying
what it *is not*. To begin with, to suppose, as many
people do suppose, that athletics and physical culture
are the same thing is quite a mistaken notion. Then is
physical culture opposed to athletics? Certainly not.
Cricket and football and rowing and swimming, and,

B 2

indeed, all forms of manly sport and exercise, are admirable things in their way, but they are not physical culture. A part of it, if you like; but physical culture is something far wider in its scope, infinitely loftier in its ideals.

What was the ideal of the Greeks? They were ardent athletes, but their pastimes were only regarded as a means to an end. The Greeks regarded the culture of the body as a sacred duty; their aim was to bring it to the highest possible state of power and beauty, and we know how they succeeded. Surely what they succeeded in doing cannot be impossible for us.

Does the reader now begin to get a clearer idea of what is meant by physical culture? As I have previously said, it is to the body what culture, in the accepted sense of the word, is to the mind. To constantly and persistently cultivate the whole of the body so that at last it shall be capable of anything that sound organs and perfectly developed muscles can accomplish—that is physical culture. The production, in short, of an absolutely perfect body—that is physical culture. To undo the evil for which civilization, and all the drawbacks it has brought in its train, have been responsible in making man regard his body lightly—that is the aim of physical culture. I think I am justified in saying that while it embraces every variety of athletics it goes very much further.

Possibly there are people who will refuse to admit that this aim is in itself a desirable one. They may say that the sound body is only valuable in so far as it enables the sound mind to perform its work. This I regard as nonsensical cant. I absolutely and strenuously refuse to allow for an instant that the cultivation of the body is, *per se*, a comparatively valueless thing. On the contrary, I maintain that he who neglects his body—and not to cultivate it *is* to neglect it—is guilty of the worst sin; for he sins against Nature. I take my stand upon this then—that the care of the body is in itself an absolutely good thing, and its neglect is no more to be excused than is the neglect of the opportunities of mental advancement which have been placed in a man's way. I am quite aware that it takes a very long time to thoroughly free ourselves from the trammels of old-established prejudice. I am quite prepared to hear of some worthy folk gravely shaking their heads and deprecating any great amount of attention being paid to the body as likely to engender undue vanity and self-esteem. I do not think that is likely to be so, but even if it should be the case I do not hold it to be such a grievous matter. If a man has striven his utmost to make the best of himself a certain amount of pride in the fact may well be forgiven him. Or, at all events, we can look upon his failing with the eye of charity.

I do not think I can conclude this chapter better than by reprinting some remarks on the subject which I wrote in the first number of " Physical Culture," my monthly magazine. The article was carefully thought out, and I do not think there is any need for me to add to it. " For after all, why should not a man feel some pride in a healthy and well-cared-for body ? Though I contend that it in itself is emphatically a good thing, that is not to say the effects of physical culture are confined to the body. In bringing the body to its highest pitch of perfection, various moral qualities, the value of which it would be difficult to over-estimate, must necessarily be brought into play. The first essential to success is the power of concentrating the will upon the work. Muscles are not developed by muscular action alone. Physical exertion, however arduous and long continued, will not make a man strong, or the day labourer and the blacksmith would be the strongest of men. Mechanical and desultory exertion will never materially increase a man's strength. He must first learn the great secret, which ought to be no secret at all. He must use his mind. He may not be able to add a cubit to his stature, but by taking thought a man can most assuredly increase the size of his muscles, strengthen all his organs, and add to his general vitality. But he must put his mind, as well as his muscles, into the work. And by exercise and practice the will-power is greatly increased, until, in course of time, the whole organism is so absolutely under its control that the muscles can be kept in perfect condition even without what, in ordinary language, is called " exercise." That is to say, that without violent exertion, but merely by the exertion of the will, the muscles can be exercised almost to any extent. Can it for a moment be supposed that this cultivation of the will-power is not of great value to an individual, no matter what sort of task or work he may be engaged in? Is it not largely by the exercise of will-power that most things are achieved? Take two men of equal talents; give them equal opportunities; but let one's will-power and power of concentration be relatively much greater than his fellow's. Then set them to perform the same task. Which will succeed best? No person endowed with ordinary intelligence can be in doubt for a moment. Will-power is a mighty factor—perhaps the mightiest—in all that goes to make up the sum of human success or failure. But the strengthening of will· though perhaps the chief—is not by a long way the only benefit which physical culture confers. The man who means to make his body as nearly perfect as possible must perforce cultivate habits of self-control and of temperance. Not the temperance which consists of rigidly abstaining from all the 'pleasant vices,' but the *real* temperance which teaches a man to say ' No,' which teaches him to indulge in all that is conducive to happiness without being in danger of that overstepping of the boundary line which leads to misery. The man who has cultivated his body has also cultivated self-respect. He has learned the virtue and the happiness of rigid personal cleanliness; his views of life are sane and wholesome. Respecting himself he learns to respect others. He is gentle, and only uses his powers against his fellowmen when called upon to do so in the defence of the oppressed and helpless. It is your weakling who is generally a bully and a tyrant. To take a few men who are exceptionally endowed by Nature, to make them extraordinarily strong, and to then train them to perform particular feats, is not a thing very difficult of accomplishment. But that is not the aim of physical culture. Its ultimate object is to raise the average standard of the race as a whole. That is, no doubt, a stupendous task, and one which it may take many lifetimes to accomplish. But everything must have its beginning, and unless we set about improving the physique of the present generation, we cannot hope to benefit those who come after us. Healthier and more perfect men and women will beget children with better constitutions and more free from hereditary taint. They in their turn, if the principles and the duty of physical culture are early instilled into them, will grow up more perfect types of men and women than were their mothers and fathers. So the happy progression will go on, until, who knows, if in the days to come there will not be a race of mortals walking this earth of ours even surpassing those who, according to the old myth, were the offspring of the union of the sons of the gods with the daughters of men! That is, perhaps, an almost impossible ideal, but it is well to set one's ideals high. Surely what has been done for the horse and the dog cannot be impossible of accomplishment in the case of man. At all events, it is worth trying."

To wind up this chapter with a word of encouragement to those who come quite fresh to the subject; to those who in taking up Physical Culture are venturing into what is to them unexplored territory—"Read, think, and work. Do not be disheartened because your progress at first seems slow; nothing worth having is to be won without labour. I can only tell you what to do, only point out to you the right road. The rest lies with yourself. I should be the sorriest humbug · if I endeavoured to make you believe otherwise, and you would be the simplest of fools if you *did* believe me. There is no royal road to success, and a very bad thing would it be if there were. For your reward lies not so much in the accomplishment as in the effort and struggle, and all the good qualities which they bring out."

CHAPTER II.

THE PROGRESS OF THE SYSTEM.

I have already remarked upon the satisfactory progress which the system has made during the last few
years. It is probably well-known that my system has
practically been adopted in the Army; although the
method adopted in the Army gymnasia is not absolutely
identical with that which I advocate, it is obviously
based upon the same principles. People may be
interested to hear that since I opened my first school,
some eighteen months ago, amongst my pupils have
been a great number of gentlemen, who, desirous of
adopting the Army as a career, have been unable to do
so through not coming up to the physical standpoint
required. In many cases they have actually been
rejected on this account; in others they have been
fearful that such might be their fate, and have come to
me in order to avoid it. Some have not been heavy
enough for their height; others lacking in chest
measurement, and so on. Now let my system be judged
by the results. *In not a single instance have I failed to
do what is necessary.* That may stand by itself without
any further comment from me. However, as a further
proof of the efficacy of the system, I may say that I have
put an *inch* on the *height* of a young fellow in *three
weeks!* This may sound incredible, but it is an absolute
fact. The majority of these gentlemen, whom I have
helped to pass the Army "medical," have written me
appreciative letters, and though for obvious reasons I
cannot publish them, I shall be happy to show them to
any reader who may care to call at the St. James'-street

school. That the value of the system is fully recognised in the Army is demonstrated by the letter from Colonel Fox, late inspector of the Army Gymnasia, which appears in this book. Amongst the civilian public the system is spreading rapidly; private individuals are taking it up and working steadily in their own homes, whilst in a great number of gymnasia throughout the country, classes are being formed to carry it out. In connection with this, it is highly diverting to notice that various individuals who are never tired of denouncing me and all my works, have set up as "professors" of physical culture, and are actually teaching my system! Of course they would be loth to admit this, and would assert that it is a system of their own. All I can say is that by a strange coincidence nearly every one of these systems which I have examined is based upon the same principles as my own. Now that I have made mention of those who try to gain notoriety by attacking my system, I cannot refrain from commenting upon certain statements which, having been widely circulated, may tend to do the system injury. The subject is, I think, worthy of a short chapter to itself.

CHAPTER III.

THE STUPIDITY OF ENVY.

The statement to which I refer is this — that
though by my system a man may increase the size
of his muscles, add to his bodily strength, and improve
his physique, he does so at the expense of his vital
organs. This statement has been freely bandied about
by those who ought to be above such petty and stupid
malice ; men, who, professing to teach physical culture,
are mostly quite ignorant of the very rudiments of the
subject. Their reasons for such utterances are not far
to seek ; they are envious of the success which has
attended the years of hard work and endeavour I have
gone through, and regard me as a rival to damage whom
everything is justifiable. One or two have even gone so
far as to say that I myself am anything but sound, that
my heart is in a very bad condition, and that there is
every probability of my " going over to the majority " at
a very early age.

Let me nail these outrageous lies to the counter once
and for all. Some who repeat them doubtless do so in
good faith ; let them listen and amend their ways. For
those who circulated them, well knowing them to be
false, I have no words in which to express my contempt.
Fair and square opposition I can face ; but a lie, however groundless, once sent on its journey is difficult to
overtake.

Now for my refutation. First, amongst my pupils
have been many who, prior to coming to me, had been
rejected as unsound by Life Insurance Companies ; well,
they have got their policies safely locked up now. Some

had weak hearts, some poor lungs, others were generally unfit. They came to me, generally, for two or three months, applied again, and were accepted. Those who doubt my word can, as in the case of the Army lads, see the proofs for themselves. Is that good enough, or does "our friend, the enemy," require any further demonstration that, far from injuring the vital organs, in many cases my system is enormously beneficial to those who are delicate. If so, here it is. They say *I* am unsound; very well, here is an answer for them.

Some months ago I was insured for a large sum in the Norwich Union Life Insurance Company; I was accepted in the *highest class*, and the doctor who saw me expressed great surprise at the soundness of my heart, the strength of my lungs, and in fact at the fine condition of all my organs. Surely these envious people show little ingenuity in inventing falsehoods which can be so easily disproved.

CHAPTER IV.

HOW TO EXERCISE.

In commencing the system of exercises described and illustrated by the anatomical chart, there are certain questions which every student naturally asks himself.

Probably the very first of these questions is, "What part of the day ought I to devote to these exercises?"

The answer to this question must depend on the pupil himself—on his leisure and on his inclination. Some persons find the early morning the best and most convenient time; others prefer the afternoon; and a third class, again, find that they feel best, and have the most leisure, at night. I do not, therefore, lay down a hard and fast rule of time. The golden rule is to select such part of the day as suits you best, always avoiding exercise immediately after meals. If possible, let two hours elapse between a meal and exercise. Moreover, do not exercise just before going to bed if you find it has a tendency to keep you awake. Many of my pupils find that they sleep much better after exercise; but there are some upon whom it has a reverse effect.

If possible, the pupil should always exercise stripped to the waist; if he wear a singlet it should be cut well away round the arms, so as to allow of free play for the muscles around the shoulder. It is also desirable to exercise before a looking-glass, for then the movements of the various muscles can be followed, and to see the muscles at work, and to mark their steady development, is itself a help and a pleasure.

In performing the exercises the pupil should bend the knees slightly and keep the muscles of the thighs tense; the legs will thus share in the benefit of all the movements.

What I wish to impress on delicate pupils is the desirability of progress by degrees. Many men before beginning my system of physical training have been so weak that doctors have thought little of the prospect of saving their lives, yet to-day they are amongst the strongest. They have progressed gradually, always being careful not to undertake too much, and thus to adapt the exercises to their own individual requirements. It may be mentioned also that the old, as well as the young, may derive great benefits from my system, though all who are over the age of fifty should moderate the exercises on the lines suggested in the table of ages for pupils between fifteen and seventeen. My exercises will also be found of considerable benefit to persons who suffer from obesity.

Pupils must not be discouraged because, after the first few days' training, they may feel stiff. It sometimes happens that a young man or woman, or perhaps a middle-aged one, sets out on the course of training with the greatest enthusiasm. After the first two or three days the enthusiasm, perhaps, wears off. Then comes a period of stiffness, and the pupil is inclined to think that he cannot be bothered to proceed with the course. To such pupils, I would say, in all earnestness, "Don't be overcome by apparent difficulties; if you wish to succeed, go forward; never draw back." This stiffness, moreover, becomes a very pleasant feeling. You soon grow to like it; personally, indeed, it may be said that it is one of the most agreeable sensations I have ever had.

Frequently pupils ask me how long it should take them to get strong. The answer again depends on themselves, not only on their physical constitution, but also on the amount of will power they put into their exercises. As I have said already, it is the brain that developes the muscles. Brain will do as much as dumb-bells, even more. For example, when you are sitting down reading, practise contracting your muscles. Do this every time you are sitting down leisurely, and by contracting them harder and harder each time, you will find that it will have the same effect as the use of dumb-bells or any more vigorous form of exercise.

It is very advisable for all pupils to get into the habit of constantly practising this muscle-contraction. In itself it is an admirable exercise, but it is perhaps even more valuable owing to the fact that it improves the will power and helps to establish that connection between the brain and the muscles which is the basis of strength and " condition."

It will be noticed that throughout my exercises I make a point of alternate movements. By this means one arm, or, as the case may be, one set of muscles, is given a momentary rest whilst the other is in motion, and thus freer circulation is gained than by performing the movements simultaneously and the strain upon the heart and lungs relieved.

Another question which pupils are constantly asking me is whether it is right for them to perspire after the exercises. The answer to this question is that it depends on the constitution of the pupil. If you perspire, it does you good; if you do not it shows that your condition is sound already. Of course it will be understood that I am answering in this, as in other questions, for general cases. There are always exceptions.

Again, " What," it is asked, " are the general benefits of the Sandow system of physical training ? "

The benefits are not, of course, confined to the visible muscular development. The inner organs of the body also share them. The liver and kidneys are kept in good order, the heart and nerves are strengthened, the brain and energy are braced up. The body, in fact, like a child, wants to be educated, and only through a series of exercises can this education be given. By its aid the whole body is developed and, as will be seen, pupils who have conscientiously worked at my system testify freely to the good results obtained, not only in the direction of vastly increasing their muscular strength, but of raising the standard of their vitality and general health.

For the beginner the most difficult part of my system is so fully to concentrate his mind on his muscles as to get them absolutely under control. It will be found, however, that this control comes by degrees. The brain sends a message to the muscles; the nerves receive it, and pass it on to them. With regard to the will power that is exerted it should be remembered that whilst the effect of weight lifting is to contract the muscles, the same effect is produced by merely contracting the muscles without lifting the weight.

This question of "will power" has, I am aware, troubled a good many of my pupils. The majority find it difficult to " put all they know " into movements with small dumb-bells, and consequently are apt to be disappointed at the results of their work. Not infrequently I have received a letter stating that the writer is doing the exercises an immense number of times, occupying several hours a day—three or four or even more!—and yet does not find that there is very much improvement. The reason is obvious; he is simply " going through " the motions and not really working at them. On the other hand, here and there, I come across a man possessing an amount of will power out of all proportion to his strength. The consequence is that he soon gets exhausted, and either cannot get through his exercises or only does so at the cost of becoming thoroughly done up and jaded. The great rule that progress in the direction of the exertion of will power should be gradual and ever continuing, is one that many people confess they are unable to carry out.

Now I have for long been perplexed to find a means of remedying this, and at last I think I have discovered a method whereby the amount of will-power exerted by the pupil can be regulated. In the next chapter particulars are given of my new " Grip " Dumb-bell, which I think ought to prove a veritable godsend to all, and especially to those to whom reference has just been made.

CHAPTER V.

MY "GRIP" DUMB-BELL.

This appliance is very simple and may be described in a few words. It consists of a dumb-bell made in two halves separated about an inch and a half from one another, the intervening space being occupied by a small steel spring. When exercising, the spring is compressed by gripping the bells and bringing the two halves close together, in which position they are kept until the exercise is over. The springs can be of any strength, and consequently the power necessary to keep the two halves together can be varied to any extent.

The advantages of this arrangement are obvious. Whether he will or no, the pupil *must grip* the bells hard, and as the strength of the springs are known he can regulate his progress to a nicety as he grows stronger. There is also another point in connection with the new device to which I want to draw particular attention. It will often happen that a pupil who is exercising will feel " a bit off-colour " one day, and consequently less inclined to exercise, or he may be worried and perplexed by his business affairs to a degree which renders it almost impossible for him to concentrate his mind solely upon the work. The natural consequence of either of these two conditions is that unless he possess very uncommon will power, if he is exercising with ordinary bells, he only does so in a desultory and half-hearted manner, and benefits little thereby. Now this is impossible with the " grip " bell—however pre-occupied and worried the pupil may be he has a definite point upon which to concentrate his mind; he *must* exert a certain amount of force in gripping the bells to keep the two halves together, and consequently *must* put out a certain amount of will-power.

Of course there is no reason why in using the "grip" dumb-bells, only the grip necessary to keep the two halves together should be exerted. On the contrary, as with ordinary bells, a man may, and should put "all he knows" into the work; the special point and the great merit about the former is that with them the amount of power exerted can never fall below a known and easily regulated *minimum*.

The pupil who possesses these bells will find that instead of having to be continually buying heavier dumb-bells, one pair will suffice him for all time. All that it will be necessary for him to do will be to purchase, at a small expense, new springs from time to time. All pupils are advised to use the dumb-bell, upon the merits of which I need not further enlarge. As will have been seen, this is not a mechanical device which will render unnecessary the employment of will-power; that would be opposed to all my theories and teaching. On the contrary it will aid in developing will-power, as it will stimulate the pupil to put it forth, and guide him how to use it in the proper direction.

CHAPTER VI.

THE MAGIC COLD BATH.

I am sometimes accused of being a bit of a faddist about the use of the cold bath, and possibly the heading of this chapter may give strength to that opinion. But its exhilarating and health-giving effects really justify the use of the adjective. The longer I live, and the greater my experience, the more am I convinced of its virtues. Let me advise every pupil after exercising, while the body is still hot, to take a cold bath. It does not matter how much he may be perspiring; the cold bath will prove exceedingly beneficial. He must be careful, however, not to take his bath if he is out of breath. The exercises will, no doubt, quicken the heart's action; but in from three to five minutes after the series is completed, the heart should be beating normally again. For persons who suffer from weak heart I should not advise a cold bath. As a general rule there is no need to ask the question, "Is my heart weak?" For if it is weak you should know it beyond a doubt. After every little exertion, though the assertion may appear paradoxical, you will feel it beating in your head.

In advising cold baths, I speak, of course, for persons in the enjoyment of ordinary health. The bath should be begun in the summer and continued every morning throughout the year. In the winter, if the room is cold, light the gas and close the window. If your hair is not injuriously affected by cold water—and in many cases, I believe, cold water will be found to strengthen it— begin, as you stand over the bath, by splashing the water five and twenty times over your head. In any case, if you are averse to wetting the hair, be careful to begin by sponging the temples and nape of the neck. Next, whilst still standing over the bath, splash the water fifteen times against the chest and ten times against the heart. Then jump into the bath, going right down under the water. In the summer you may remain in the water from ten to fifteen seconds, but in the winter let it be just a jump in and out again.

The subsequent rub down with towels is popularly supposed to produce half the benefits that result from a cold bath. I have no hesitation in saying that this is a great mistake. Let me explain the reason : As you get out of the bath you rub down first one part of the body and then the other, and thus, whilst the one part is being warmed by the friction, the other is getting cold. Many people who take cold baths in this way complain of touches of rheumatism, and the whole trouble arises, I believe, from different parts of the body being alternately warmed and chilled.

In order to overcome the risk of this ill-effect my advice is this : Do not spend any time over rubbing yourself down. If you do not like the idea of getting into your clothes wet, just take the water off the body as quickly as you possibly can with a dry towel, jump into your clothes, and let Nature restore your circulation in her own way. You will get quite as warm by this method as by vigorously rubbing down, with the added advantage that the heat of the body will be more evenly distributed. If, owing to poor health or other exceptional causes, the circulation is not fully and promptly restored, walk briskly up and down the room. If you should still feel cold in any part of the body probably the bath is not suited to your constitution, and in that case it is not advised. In ninety-nine cases out of a hundred, however, the cold bath, taken as I have described, will have nothing but the most beneficial effects; and, if taken every morning throughout the year, it is the surest preventive that I know against catching cold. On the other hand, irregularity is liable

to produce cold. In short, having once begun the cold
bath, make a rule, summer and winter, never to leave
it off.

Personally, I find the very best form of the cold bath
is to get into your clothes after it without drying the
body at all. For the first moment or two the sensation
may not be perfectly agreeable, but afterwards you feel
better and warmer for adopting this method. The damp
is carried away through the clothes and no particle of
wet is left.

For pupils who have not the convenience of a bathroom a cold sponging down may be recommended as a
substitute. In this case let two towels be taken and
soaked with water. Rub the front of the body down
with one, and the back with the other. This method
prevents the towel from absorbing the heat from the
body, and the cold sponging is thus distributed evenly
over its surface. Afterwards dry the body quickly as
before, letting no time be lost in getting into your
clothes.

I have often been asked whether in the event of
exercising at night it is advisable to take a cold bath
afterwards. My reply is :—" certainly." *Always* have a
cold bath or sponge down after exercising. It will make
you feel " as fresh as paint," improve your appetite, and
make the skin clean and firm, and be generally conducive
to happiness and good health. Some people tell me
that a cold bath immediately before retiring keeps them
awake; if that be so, I should advise them to exercise
earlier in the day. But the exercise and the cold bath
ought to be regarded as inseparable.

CHAPTER VII.

PHYSICAL CULTURE FOR THE MIDDLE-AGED.

It is scarcely necessary for me to say that the benefits to be obtained by conscientiously working upon my system are by no means confined to the young and vigorous. On the contrary, it is particularly suitable for the middle-aged, who are all too apt to suffer from the effects of the period of physical indolence which has succeeded their youthful activity. To such, the system should prove invaluable. It is quite a false notion to suppose that when once youth is passed exercise is no longer necessary. *So long as life lasts, if an individual wants to keep healthy, exercise is just as necessary as food.* It is through neglecting to recognise this that so many men become aged before their time. When a man begins to get into middle life he has a natural tendency to "take things easy." He lives more luxuriously, devotes more time to the pleasures of the table, and exerts himself as little as possible. Is it anything to wonder at that his health suffers, that he grows fat and flabby, and that his digestive apparatus quickly gets out of gear? If in his youth he has been an athlete the more will his changed mode of life tell upon him; it is indeed better never to have exercised at all than to exercise for a few years and then drop it entirely. It is for this reason we hear of the health of so many athletes failing them at a comparatively early age. And this failure is, as a rule, erroneously ascribed to the effects upon their constitution of their early efforts. Once and again errors in "training" may be responsible for poor health in middle-age, but in ninety-nine cases out of a hundred the complete cessation from active bodily work, combined with the greater indulgence which naturally follows, is alone responsible.

Of course, while it is advisable that the middle-aged man should exercise regularly, I must warn him not to do too much. He must remember that what is perfectly safe and prudent at five-and-twenty may be rash and hazardous at fifty; in short, that he, while exercising consistently and steadily, must be careful not to over-tax his powers. If he bears this in mind he will find that the discomforts and ailments which he has perhaps got to regard as natural to his time of life are quickly banished, and that, in spite of his grey beard and thinning hair, it is still " good to be alive."

CHAPTER VIII.

PHYSICAL CULTURE FOR WOMEN.

I am exceedingly anxious to remove the impression, which has, I fear, gained ground, that my system is not a thing for women. Now-a-days, when women have practically freed themselves from the antiquated ideas of a generation or so ago, there ought to be small difficulty in convincing them that to make the best of themselves, in a physical sense, is just as imperative a duty for them as for their brothers. Women go in for all sorts of sports and pastimes to-day; they bicycle, row, play tennis and hockey, and not infrequently display no small degree of excellence in sports which have hitherto been regarded as " for men only." This is a hopeful sign, but I am not at all sure that in many cases it is not more provocative of harm than good. Women are possessed of a great amount of nervous energy, and, unless their bodies and organs are gradually and systematically trained to bear exertion and fatigue, they are likely to attempt performances which are quite beyond their physical power, although, buoyed up as they are by a fund of nervous energy and mental exhilaration, they may observe no ill-effects at the time. This is one reason why it is so advisable for women to commence by working upon my system, which is so mild and gradual that they can pursue it without any risks, and, while daily growing stronger and healthier, be scarcely conscious that they are making any effort whatever.

I am quite aware that there is a very wide-spread notion that exercise tends to coarsen and render a woman unbeautiful, but that is absolutely false. Were there any truth in it I should indeed despair of converting my fair readers to my way of thinking, for truly it is woman's mission to look beautiful. But the idea is absurd; Nature, which intended woman to look lovely, also intended her to be healthy; indeed, the two are practically synonymous. Of course, improper, violent and one-sided exercise will naturally result in making a woman clumsy, heavy, and ungraceful, but proper exercise, having for its object symmetrical and perfect development, will have an exactly contrary effect. Curiously enough, the visible effect of proper exercise upon a woman's muscles is not precisely the same as upon those of a man. Regular and gradually progressive exercise will not make a woman's muscles prominent, but will cause them to grow firm and round and impart to the outline of the figure those graceful contours which are so universally admired. Without well-conditioned muscle the most beautifully proportioned woman in the world will look comparatively shapeless and flabby; her muscles are not required to show up as in the case of a man's, but they must be there all the same as a solid foundation for the overlying flesh. Take a woman's arm, for instance; if it has been duly exercised and developed, it is easy enough to see that its shapeliness and good modelling are due to the muscles; white and soft though the skin may be, you can tell at a glance that it is firm and elastic to the touch. On the other hand, the arm of the woman who has never exercised the muscles, betrays the fact unmistakably; it may be plump and round, but its lines are lacking in beauty, its movements in grace; and so with the figure generally.

The effects of my system are very rapidly noticeable. It reduces the size of the waist, makes the limbs round, the figure pliant, the walk and carriage graceful and easy. For those women who are doomed to a more or less sedentary life it works wonders, and those whose means and occupation permit of their indulging in a healthier outdoor life will find it a splendid preparation for their favourite pastimes.

Just a word with regard to complexion. A fine skin and a good healthy colour are the best proofs of the possession of good health. Indeed, without health a good skin and complexion are out of the question; and where is the woman who does not desire to possess both? She is indeed rare. Therefore, to those women who, while they do not set a high enough value upon health and strength for their own sakes, yet desire to be fair to look upon, I say the two things must inevitably go hand in hand. Whether your prime object be to obtain beauty or health does not matter; by working upon my system you will obtain both.

CHAPTER IX.

THE TABLES OF AGES.

From the following tables pupils of all ages will be able to see at a glance how many times the movements of each exercise illustrated by the anatomical chart should be practised daily.

It should be clearly understood that the tables are only intended as a guide, and that they are not intended to arbitrarily fix the amount of work which the pupil should do. It is an absolute impossibility to lay down rules which will suit every individual case, and consequently pupils must, after taking the table as a basis, use their own discretion as to how they shall vary them. The great thing to bear in mind is to proceed very gradually; while exercising, put "all you know" into the work, but don't attempt to do too much. Exercise until the muscles ache, but never go on to the point of feeling thoroughly "blown" and exhausted. A quarter of an hour's conscientious work is better than an hour spent in "going through the motions" in a desultory fashion. Pupils who are in any difficulty and wish for special guidance are advised to go in for the 2s. 6d. course of instruction by post which is given in connection with "Physical Culture," full particulars of which are given in this book. As I have already said, I should advise all pupils to use the "Grip" dumb-bell; then, instead of buying a heavier pair of dumb-bells after the exercises are being done a certain number of times, all that will be necessary will be to use a stronger spring. I do not advise pupils to keep on with the same weight bells or the same spring too long; when the exercises are done a very great number of times the work becomes monotonous and there is a natural tendency to do it in a mechanical manner. Roughly speaking, when it takes much over half-an-hour to get through the whole series it is desirable to begin again with heavier bells or springs.

Parents who desire to see their little ones grow into well-developed men and women may be advised to buy their babies light wooden dumb-bells as playthings. The exercises themselves, of course, should not be attempted until the child has reached the age of six or seven. Parents especially would do well to remember, as has already been said, that the tables are only intended as a guide, and they should exercise their own discretion with regard to the weight of bells used by their children, and the number of times the exercises should be done. In some cases a girl or boy of ten years may be so delicate as to have no more strength than a more sturdy child two or three years younger; in such cases the table for the younger child should be adhered to. From that age onwards be guided in the amount of practice by the tables. In order that every reader may understand the exercises easily, the leading muscles only are mentioned in the chart.

Pupils should guard against over-exertion; and, above all things, should not exercise violently. It will be found convenient to let each arm (not both arms) move once in a second. Thus, for example, the time of ten movements with each arm of the first exercise would be twenty seconds. As a general rule, this time will be found to give just the exercise that is needed. Faster movements are not recommended for either young or old. Be careful also not to jerk the movements. Always exercise easily and gracefully, and when contracting the muscles take care *not to hold the breath.* Many pupils are inclined to do this unconsciously when bringing their minds to bear upon the muscles, but it is quite wrong, and the tendency must be striven against until it is overcome. In one or two exercises, as will be seen on the chart, there are special instructions with regard to the breath; in all the others the breathing should be perfectly natural.

TABLE 1.

FOR CHILDREN OF BOTH SEXES

BETWEEN THE AGES OF SEVEN AND TEN.

(Using one pound dumb-bells only.)

When the *maximum* has been reached, the child should *continue* to use the same weight bells and the same spring in the "Grip" dumb-bell until it arrives at the age at which it can follow Table No. 2, and so on with the other tables.

No. of Exercise. (See Chart.)		No. of Movements with each arm.		Increase of Movements. (Not to exceed 30 for No. 1, and other Exercises in proportion.)
1	......	10	......	One every three days.
2	......	5	......	„ „ „
3	......	5	......	„ „ „
4	......	4	......	One every five days.
5	......	4	......	„ „ „
6	......	10	......	One every three days.
7	......	6	......	One every five days.

Exercises 8, 9, and 10 are not advised
for young children.

11	......	5	......	One every five days.
12	......	5	......	„ „ „
13	......	1	......	One every fortnight.
14	......	5	......	One every three days.
15	......	3	......	One every fortnight.
16 (boys only)		3	......	„ „ „
17	......	10	......	One every three days.
18	......	10	......	„ „

TABLE 2.

FOR CHILDREN OF BOTH SEXES
BETWEEN THE AGES OF TEN AND TWELVE.

(Using two pound dumb-bells only.)

No. of Exercise.		No. of Movements.	Increase of Movements. (Not to exceed 40 for No. 1, and other Exercises in proportion.)
1	......	10	...... One every three days.
2	......	5	...... „ „ „
3	......	5	...... „ „ „
4	......	4	...... One every five days.
5	......	4	...... „ „ „
6	......	10	...... One every three days.
7	......	6	...... One every five days.

Exercises 8, 9, and 10 are not advised.

11	.....	5	...... One every five days.
12	......	5	...... „ „ „
13	......	1	...... One every fortnight.
14	......	6	...... One every three days.
15	......	3	...... One every fortnight.

Exercises 16 and 17 are not advised.

16	(boys only)	3	...... One every fortnight.
17	......	10	...... One every three days
18	......	10	...... „ „ „

TABLE 3.

FOR CHILDREN OF BOTH SEXES

BETWEEN THE AGES OF TWELVE AND FIFTEEN.

(Using three pound dumb-bells only.)

No of Exercise.		No. of Movements.	Increase of Movements. (Not to exceed 50 for No. 1, and other Exercises in proportion.)
1	......	10	...... One every three days.
2	......	5	...... „ „ „
3	......	5	...... „ „ „
4	......	4	...... One every five days.
5	......	4	...... „ „ ,
6	......	10	...... One every three days.
7	......	6	...... One every five days.

Exercises 8, 9, and 10 are not advised.

11	......	5	...... One every five days.
12	......	5	...... „ „ „
13	......	1	...... One every fortnight.
14	......	6	...... One every three days.
15	......	3	...... One every fortnight.
16	(boys only)	3	...... „ „ „
17	......	15	...... One every three days
18	......	10	.. ... „ „ „

TABLE 4.

FOR GIRLS

BETWEEN THE AGES OF FIFTEEN AND SEVENTEEN.

(Using three pound dumb-bells only.)

No. of Exercise.		No. of Movements.		Increase of Movements. (Not to exceed 60 for No. 1, and other Exercises in proportion.)
1	......	15	......	One every three days.
2	......	8	......	„ „ „
3	......	6	......	„ „ „
4	......	6	......	One every five days.
5	......	4	......	„ „ „
6	......	10	......	One every three days.
7	......	8	......	One every five days.

Exercises 8, 9, and 10 are not advised.

No. of Exercise.		No. of Movements.		Increase of Movements.
11	......	5	......	One every five days.
12	......	5	......	„ „ „
13	......	1	......	One every fortnight.
14	......	8	......	One every three days.
15	......	3	......	One every fortnight.

Exercise 16 is not advised.

No. of Exercise.		No. of Movements.		Increase of Movements.
17	......	15	......	One every fortnight.
18	......	15	......	„ „ three days

Table 5.

For Boys

Between the Ages of Fifteen and Seventeen.

(Using at first three-pound dumb-bells.)

At this age boys, when they have increased the number of movements of the first exercise from 30 to 60, and all others in proportion, are recommended to go through the course again with five pound dumb-bells.

No. of Exercise.		No. of Movements.		Increase of Movements.
1	......	30	......	One every other day.
2	......	15	......	One every three days.
3	......	10	......	,, ,,
4	......	8	......	,, ,,
5	......	5	......	One every three days.
6	......	12	......	One every three days.
7	......	8	......	One every three days.

Exercises 8, 9, and 10 are not advised.

11	......	5	......	One every two days.
12	......	5	......	,, ,,
13	......	2	......	One a week.
14	......	15	......	One every other day.
15	......	3	......	One every three days.
16	......	3	......	One every fortnight.
17	......	25	......	One every three days.
18	......	25	......	,, ,,

TABLE 6.

FOR GIRLS.

OF SEVENTEEN YEARS OF AGE AND UPWARDS.

(Using three-pound dumb-bells only.)

No. of Exercise.		No. of Movements.	Increase of Movements. (Not to exceed 80 for No. 1 and other exercises in proportion).
1	......	20	...... One every other day.
2	......	10	...... One every three days.
3	......	7	...... „ „ „
4	......	7	...... „ „ „
5	......	4	...... One every three days.
6	......	10	...... One every two days.
7	......	8	...... One every three days.

8, 9, and 10 until the pupil feels tired.

11	......	5	...... One every two days.
12	......	5	...... „ „ „
13	......	1	...... One a week.
14	......	10	...... One every three days.
15	......	3	...... „ „ „

Exercise 16 is not advised.

| 17 | ...... | 20 | ...... One every three days |
| 18 | ...... | 20 | ... - , „ „ |

D

TABLE 7.

FOR YOUTHS.

OF SEVENTEEN YEARS OF AGE AND UPWARDS.

(Using at first four-pound dumb-bells.)

When the pupil has increased the number of movements of No. 1 to 80. he should keep at the maximum with the same weight dumb-bells for six months ; he may then increase 1lb., beginning the course over again, and so on every six months.   The heaviest bells used, however, should not exceed 10lbs.

I am aware that in the former edition of the book I placed 20lbs. as the limit, but the experience gained in my schools has taught me that for the *majority* of men this is far too heavy.   It is always better to use bells too light than too heavy ; the latter are liable to cause strains and other injuries.

No. of Exercise.		No. of Movements.		Increase of Movements.
1	......	50	......	Five every day.
2	......	25	......	Two every day.
3	......	10	......	One every day.
4	......	10	......	One every three days.
5	......	5	......	One every two days.
6	... ..	15	......	,, ,, ,,
7	......	10	......	,, ,, ,,

8, 9, and 10 until the pupil feels tired.

11	......	10	......	One every two days.
12	......	10	......	,, ,, ,,
13	......	3	......	One every three days.
14	......	25	......	Two every day.
15	......	3	......	One every two days.

CHAPTER X.

MY SCHOOLS OF PHYSICAL CULTURE.

The reader of the second part of this book will see how my professional career was thrust upon me. It came through no seeking of my own, after my defeat of Samson. I accepted it partly because the offers seemed too good to be thrown away, and partly because they enabled me to gratify a wish to see something of the world. My ambition, however, was always to form and build up a system for the service of others, rather than exhibit merely the results of that system in my own person. That ambition, I hope, is to be realised, for I have founded several schools of training for men, women, and children of both sexes, and in the course of time, I intend to establish branches in every important town.

The schools are conducted entirely on my own system of physical culture. Instruction is given by specially qualified teachers, and every exercise is lucidly described and clearly demonstrated. The pupils have every opportunity of developing their bodies to the highest extent, and from time to time I personally examine them.

The instructors employed in the school have been specially trained for their work by me, so that the pupils have the benefit of my best information, and of thus learning the whole of my system exactly. In addition to the classes for men, women, and children, arrangements are made for giving private lessons when required.

My brother-in-law, Mr. Warwick Brookes, jun., is the best pupil I have ever had. For the past six years he has followed my system thoroughly, and the results have been remarkable. When I first met him he was exceedingly

delicate.   He could only walk with the aid of crutches.
Gradually, however, he began to improve, and under my
personal supervision, by the help of my system, his strength
has so increased that to-day he is like a new man.

By means of the schools I hope to do something to sub-
stantially aid the physical development of this and succeed
ing generations.   Letters from past pupils testify to the
great benefits which can be derived from careful training
under my system, and if the training has the further
advantage of individual instruction those benefits should be
increased even more than by studying this book.

It is a pleasant ambition to hope by one's efforts to leave
the world just a little better here and there than one found
it ; and that has always been and is my ambition.   My
pupils can help me to realise it.

As I have said, I intend opening schools in every large
town in the country ; at present schools are open at the
following addresses :—

LONDON
- 32, St. James's Street, S.W.
- 115A, Ebury Street, S.W.
- Walbrook, City, E.C.
- Tottenham Court Road, W.
- Crystal Palace, S.E.

MANCHESTER :—Oxford Street.

CHAPTER XI.

INSTRUCTION BY CORRESPONDENCE.

None of my departments has shown a more gratifying development than has the correspondence department. Letters pour in from all parts of the world asking for advice and instruction in such numbers that I have been obliged to organise a special system and department for dealing with the enquiries of my many friends, who, owing to their living at a distance and to other reasons, cannot attend the schools personally.

Every week many letters reach me from the Colonies alone—from India, Canada, Australia, South Africa—even from distant Klondike—and from one and all I have received flattering testimonials as to the benefits they have derived from following my instructions. This is an example :—**Mr. Dunbar**, of Queensland, writes :—

" Dear Mr. Sandow,

" I cannot express my gratitude for the wonderful benefit " I have derived from your three months' course of instruc- " tion. Previous to practising your system I was a chronic " dyspeptic, and owing to my sedentary occupation, for many " years I had not known what it was to feel the natural " exhilaration and energy of a healthy man. Now I honestly " believe that there is not a healthier man in the whole " Colony."

One pleasing feature of this undertaking is the steady increase in the number of applications from ladies. This department has already become the most important part of my work, and anyone wishing to keep in touch with my system of Physical Culture can do so by forwarding to me their measurements, sex, age, and occupation. In the case of any physical peculiarity, or organic weakness, a doctor should be consulted, and the result of his examination stated in the letter of communication. A form is inserted at the end of this book as a guide to those wishing to apply. These forms are dealt with by myself and each case receives my individual consideration and instruction, and is signed by me.

CHAPTER XII.

SANDOW'S CHART OF MEASUREMENTS.

The figure will show pupils how to take their own measurements. They are advised to keep a careful record of these month by month, so they can see how they are progressing. The chest should be measured both with the lungs full of air and empty, as well as in its normal condition.

Date when training commenced.

....

Date on completion of course

....

Measurements then.	*Measurements now.*
Age	....
Weight	....
Height	....
Neck	....
Chest Contracted	....
Chest Expanded	....
Upper Right Arm	....
Upper Left Arm	....
Forearm, Right	....
Forearm, Left...............	....
Waist	....
Thigh, Right	....
Thigh, Left	....
Calf, Right	....
Calf, Left	....

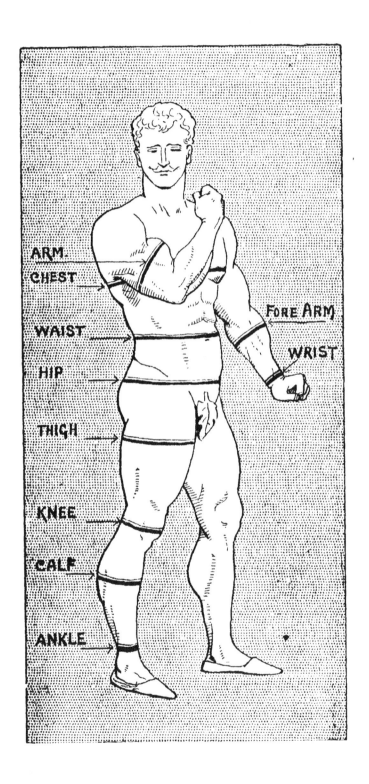

CHAPTER XIII.

THE COMBINED DEVELOPER.

After considerable experience and exhaustive experiments with rubber machines, I have succeeded in inventing one which allows of a combination of dumb-bell and rubber exercises.

Exclusive rubber exercise has not the effect of producing hard, firm, and supple muscles, therefore I have patented the detachable dumb-bell handles, which are simplicity itself.

This developer can be so regulated as to prove equally beneficial to a weak man as to myself.

From an economic point of view it stands alone, as at a small outlay a Developer can be purchased, which is sufficient for a whole family, and constitutes an entire athletic outfit.

The detachable rubbers and handles allow of the machine to be fixed up to any tension, so that as one becomes stronger, one has ample scope for gradually increasing one's strength. The fatal drawback to the ordinary rubber exerciser is that it only proves beneficial up to a certain point, and then it is not sufficient to carry one any further. Consequently one has to make another outlay in purchasing a heavier machine. My Developer has been designed to obviate this, as it can be regulated up to any strength.

The machine is simply made and easily fixed, causing no damage to the door or wall to which it is attached. There being no pulleys, no oiling is required, and there is no friction to wear out the covering of the cords. Thus the Developer is very durable.

Charts, illustrating Chest Expander, Dumb-bell and Developer exercises, together with a pair of nickel-plated dumb-bells, are given free with each machine. The dumb-bells being detachable can be used separately for the exercises as prescribed in this book. The exercises are specially arranged by myself, introducing several of the movements in my system of development which cannot be properly executed on any other machine.

In the charts are included special exercises for strengthening the legs; many pupils have found this very beneficial.

The above illustration shows the Developer as a Rubber Exerciser, Chest Expander, and Dumb-bells.

The great value of the Developer lies in the fact that it serves to render the muscles pliable, and the whole body flexible and supple. Certain movements with it, too, are difficult to perform satisfactorily with dumb-bells alone. I recommend pupils to use the dumb-bells and complete Developer alternately; by this means I find the most satisfactory results are obtained. Exercise with the rubber Developer affords a welcome change from work with the dumb-bells.

CHAPTER XIV.

HEAVY WEIGHT-LIFTING.

It is not my purpose in this book to give anything beyond general directions for lifting heavy weights. You can become thoroughly strong and enjoy perfect health by means of the series of exercises already described. Heavy weight-lifting requires personal instruction; that instruction will be given to those who may desire it at my schools. Under qualified instructors it may be pursued without the risk of danger.

Generally, however, it may be observed that to lift heavy weights it is desirable first to see what weight can be used without undue strain. Slowly raise this weight from your shoulder over your head, or, if from the ground, raise it somewhat more quickly. See how many times you are able to raise the weight first selected, and when you can perform the exercise with comparative ease, raising it, say, ten times, up to 80 lbs., six times from 80 to 100, and afterwards three times, increase the weight for the next day's exercise by five pounds. Continue this increase as you grow more capable remembering always to bring the left hand into play as well as the right; at the same time, though it should not be neglected, avoid overtaxing the left side.

The great thing to remember is to go slowly. Avoid anything like spasmodic efforts, and endeavour before trying a lift to thoroughly think out the different movements. Weight-lifting should never be practised in a confined space or where the weight cannot be readily dropped. To attempt to hold on to a weight after the balance has been lost may result in serious strains and other injuries; the pupil should practice dropping a weight from any position safely and gracefully. If the pupil bear these few hints in mind he will come to no harm, but, as I have said, weight-lifting is best left alone until it can be practised under the personal supervision of an experienced instructor.

A PLEASING TRIBUTE.

The following letter was written me by Colonel Fox, late Her Majesty's Inspector of Army Gymnasia, a gentleman to whom I am very greatly indebted for the interest he has taken for years past in my work and for the zeal he has shown in getting the system introduced into the British Army :—

The Gymnasium, Aldershot.
29th July, 1893.

Dear Mr. Sandow,

I am in receipt of your letter from New York which reached me on the 23rd instant, and am very glad to hear of your success in America. The book you speak of as being about to be published should also be very successful, and ought to do much towards making your system of physical development widely known.* Since your last visit to us here my Staff Instructors and non-commissioned officers under training have been energetically practising the light dumb-bell exercises you so kindly showed them.

I am convinced that your series of exercises are excellent and most carefully thought out, with a comprehensive view to the development of the body as a *whole*. Any man honestly following out your clear and simple instructions could not fail to enormously and rapidly improve his physique.

It is almost superfluous for me to add that you yourself, in *propria persona*, are the best possible advertisement of the merits of your system of training and developing of the human body.

---

* The book referred to is the large one which was published some years ago, and which is now out of print.

Any individual gifted with a fair amount of determination, is absolutely certain to develop his physical powers at an extraordinarily rapid rate and with the most happy results to his general health and mental powers and activity, by following with intelligence your system. As you very rightly say, it is only by bringing the brain to bear upon our exercises that we can hope to produce the best results with the shortest possible expenditure of time.

The absence of expensive and cumbrous apparatus is no small recommendation of your system, and you are thoroughly in the right when you assert that lasting muscular development, and consequent strength, can be best produced by the constant and energetic use of light dumb-bells, employed in a sound and scientific manner.

Believe me, yours very truly,
(Signed)   G. M. Fox, Lieut.-Colonel,
H.M. Inspector of Gymnasia in Great Britain.

Professor Eugen Sandow, New York, U.S.A.

LETTERS AND PHOTOGRAPHS OF PUPILS.

In the following pages will be found a selection from many thousands of letters which have been addressed to me by pupils who have already profited from my system of Physical Culture. Attention is specially directed to the measurements before and after training, showing the actual progress made in muscular development.

VACHWEN,
MARLBOROUGH ROAD,
WATFORD,
March 11th, 1899.

MR. SANDOW.
DEAR SIR,

I have just completed a course of lessons at your " School of Physical Culture," from which I have derived untold benefit. Through the greater part of last year I was so ill that for some time it was feared I might go into consumption. I was medically treated, and at length permitted by my doctor to try what your exercises would do.

I entered your School with weak heart, weak lungs, digestion sadly impaired. After three lessons, with persistent home work, I began very slowly to gain strength and an appetite, and now, at the end of my course, I am quite a new creature—full of vitality and energy.

The upper part of the lung, which was the chief cause of my trouble, is quite healed and healthy. I never know now what it is to feel pain and tightness in the bronchial tubes, from which I constantly suffered in the past. My digestive organs too are quite well.

I have gained in weight ...	...	...	7	lbs.
,,	,,	round the neck	1	in.
,,	,,	in the chest (contracted)	$3\frac{1}{2}$	ins.
,,	,,	,, ,, (expanded)...	4	ins.
,,	,,	,, forearm	$2\frac{1}{2}$	ins.
,,	,,	,, upper arm... ...	$2\frac{1}{2}$	ins.
,,	,,	in lung capacity	100	cbc. ins.

I should be quite pleased to be of use to you at any time in recommending to weak ones, who may be timid to commence the work, the immense benefit to be derived from it, by my own personal experience. I should like also to mention the very kind and careful treatment I have received both from your Manager, Mr. Clease, and the Class Instructor. They give the weak ones their particular attention, so that in working one is never over-worked.

I remain,
Yours gratefully,
MARY E. S. ADAMS.

EBURY STREET SCHOOL.

COPY OF MEASUREMENT SHEET.

Name :—MISS ADAMS.

Address :—Marlborough Road, Watford.

Result of Medical Examination :—" Very Bad."

Nature of Illness :—" The doctors say consumption."

Remarks :—" This is the weakest case I have ever had to treat."

	Before Training.	After 6 weeks.	After 3 months.	Increases.
Neck	11	... 11$\frac{3}{4}$	... 12	... 1
Chest Contracted	28	... 30$\frac{1}{2}$	... 31$\frac{1}{2}$	... 3$\frac{1}{2}$
,, Expanded	30	... 33	... 35	... 5
Upper Arm, Right	8$\frac{1}{2}$	... 10	... 11	... 2$\frac{1}{2}$
,, Left	8	... 10	... 10$\frac{1}{2}$	... 2$\frac{1}{2}$
Fore Arm, Right...	8$\frac{1}{4}$	... 9$\frac{1}{2}$	... 10$\frac{3}{4}$	.. 2$\frac{1}{2}$
,, Left ...	8$\frac{1}{4}$	... 9$\frac{1}{2}$	... 10$\frac{1}{4}$	... 2
Waist	22	... 23	... 23	... 1
Thigh, Right ...	16	... 17$\frac{1}{2}$	... 18$\frac{1}{2}$	... 2$\frac{1}{2}$
,, Left	16	... 17$\frac{1}{2}$	... 18$\frac{1}{2}$	... 2$\frac{1}{2}$
Calf, Right	10$\frac{3}{4}$	... 11$\frac{1}{4}$	... 11$\frac{3}{4}$	... 1
,, Left	10$\frac{3}{4}$	... 11$\frac{1}{4}$	... 11$\frac{3}{4}$	... 1
Height	...5ft. 6in.	...5ft. 6$\frac{1}{2}$in.	...5ft. 7in.	... 1in.
Weight... ...	...7st. 2lb	.. 7st. 8lb	...7st. 9lb	... 7lb.
Lung Capacity ...	100	... 170	... 200	... 100
Chest Expansion...	2	... 2$\frac{1}{2}$	... 3$\frac{1}{2}$	... 1$\frac{1}{2}$

57, GLOUCESTER TERRACE, W.,

March 12th, 1899.

DEAR SIR,

I am glad to take this opportunity of saying how very much my health has benefited in every way from your system of Physical Culture. It always gives me great pleasure to recommend the same to my friends.

I am,

Yours faithfully,

JULIA F. M. JOHNSTON.

E. SANDOW, ESQ.

EBURY STREET SCHOOL.

COPY OF MEASUREMENT SHEET.

Name :—MISS J. F. M. JOHNSTON.

Address :—57, Gloucester Terrace, W.

	Before Training.	After 6 weeks.	After 3 months.	Increases.
Neck	$12\frac{3}{8}$ ...	13 ...	$13\frac{1}{4}$ ...	$\frac{7}{8}$
Chest Contracted	$29\frac{1}{2}$ ...	31 ...	$31\frac{1}{2}$ ...	2
,, Expanded	32 ...	$36\frac{1}{2}$ ...	37 ...	5
Upper Arm, Right	10 ...	12 ...	$12\frac{1}{2}$ ...	$2\frac{1}{2}$
,, Left	$10\frac{1}{8}$ ...	12 ...	$12\frac{1}{2}$ ...	$2\frac{3}{8}$
Fore Arm, Right...	$9\frac{1}{2}$ ...	$10\frac{1}{4}$ ...	$10\frac{1}{2}$ ...	1
,, Left ...	$8\frac{3}{4}$ ...	$10\frac{1}{4}$ ...	$10\frac{1}{2}$ ...	$1\frac{3}{4}$
Waist	24 ...	24 ...	$24\frac{1}{2}$ ...	$\frac{1}{2}$
Thigh, Right ...	$18\frac{1}{2}$ ...	$19\frac{1}{2}$ ...	$19\frac{3}{4}$ ...	$1\frac{1}{4}$
,, Left... ...	$18\frac{1}{2}$ ...	$19\frac{1}{2}$ ...	$19\frac{3}{4}$ ...	$1\frac{1}{4}$
Calf, Right... ...	12 ...	13 ...	$13\frac{1}{4}$ ...	$1\frac{1}{4}$
,, Left	12 ...	13 ...	$13\frac{1}{4}$ ...	$1\frac{1}{4}$
Height... ...	...5ft. $4\frac{3}{8}$in....	5ft. $4\frac{3}{4}$in....	— ...	$\frac{3}{8}$
Weight ...	.. 8st. 3lb....	8st. 4lb....	8st. 6lb....	3lb.
Lung Capacity ...	200 ...	219 ...	222 ...	22
Chest Expansion..	$2\frac{1}{2}$ ...	$5\frac{1}{2}$ ...	$5\frac{1}{2}$ ...	3

THOS. A FOX.

23, Church Row,
Limehouse, E.,
December 3rd.

Mr. E. Sandow,
Dear Sir,

I write these few lines to convey to you my thanks and gratitude for the boon you have given me and the public at large. I refer to your excellent book on how to gain health, muscle, and strength.

I procured one about two years ago, and have studied and practised the drills incessantly since. The result is far beyond my expectations. I am nineteen years of age and small of stature, being only five feet in height and seven stone in weight, yet, without exaggeration, I can say that my strength and muscular development would do credit to a man six feet high.

I have gained this solely by your system and cannot praise it too highly.

Another great advantage over other systems is the small outlay required, as I have obtained for a few shillings all that is necessary to train with, whereas if I had trained under another system I should have had to have made a much larger outlay for apparatus.

I enclose a list stating what I have gained in strength and muscle since I started training.

It will always be a great pleasure to me to answer any questions concerning your system, likewise interview anyone who might be desirous of seeing me.

I remain,

Yours truly,

Thos. A. Fox.

Name :—T. A. Fox.

Address :—23, Church Row, Limehouse, E.

MEASUREMENTS.

	BEFORE TRAINING.	AFTER TRAINING.
Chest...	29 inches	32½ inches
Chest (expanded) ...	30 ,,	34 ,,
Biceps	10 ,,	13 ,,
Forearm	9½ ,,	12 ,,
Thigh	16½ ,,	20 ,,
Calf	11 ,,	13 ,,
Waist	26 ,,	26 ,,

HEAVY WEIGHT-LIFTING.

BEFORE TRAINING.

From ground above head
{ Right hand ... 56℔ dumb-bell.
Left hand .. 46℔ ,,
Both hands... 84℔ bar.'

Holding at arm's length straight from shoulder } Right hand ... 22℔ weight.
Left hand ... 20℔ ,,

After two years' training under your system.

From ground above head
{ Right hand... 100℔ dumb-bell.
Left hand ... 80℔ ,,
Both hands... 130℔ ,,

Holding at arm's length straight from shoulder } Right hand ... 40℔ weight.
Left hand ... 30℔ ,,

JOHN P. PETERS.   (Before Training.)

JOHN P. PETERS. (After Training.)

MON REPOS,

66A, HERNE HILL,

LONDON, S.E.,

March 6th.

MANAGER CLEASE,

DEAR SIR,

It is just over three years since I started to improve my physical power by means of the Sandow system, and I take this opportunity of forwarding some photographs taken at different periods. In what measure I have succeeded can best be seen by comparison of my original efforts and my present attainments, of which I also forward a list. Although they are as yet nothing to boast about or sufficiently great to be handed down to posterity, they are the result of close application to the system Mr. Sandow originated, and by means of which, in a few years, I hope to attain the culmination of human strength, and, if possible, to rival that of Sandow himself, for I am a firm believer in starting with an almost unattainable ideal, then gradually coming within measurable distance of it, and eventually, perhaps, to reach it. To do this will require the exercise of many mental qualities, determination, perseverance, and endurance. I suppose there are many young men like myself in whom Mr. Sandow has awakened a latent ambition to muscular prowess, and in doing so I state without any hesitation that he alone has done as much good for the country as any man of the present century.

I can only conclude with expressing my deep gratitude to Mr. Sandow for the splendid facilities he has offered to those who wish to be classed as nature's men (which is indeed the duty of man), and in doing so I am but echoing the sentiments of many of his pupils.

I have the honour to be,

Faithfully yours,

JOHN P. PETERS.

EBURY STREET SCHOOL.

COPY OF MEASUREMENT SHEET.

Name :—JOHN PETERS.

Address :—66a, Herne Hill, S.E.

	Before Training.	After Course.	Increase.
Neck	16	18½	2½
Chest, contracted ...	38	40	2
,, expanded ...	44	47	3
Upper Arm, Right ...	15¾	17½	1¾
,, Left ...	15	17	2
Forearm, Right ...	13	15	2
,, Left... ...	12¼	14½	2¼
Waist...	30	30	—
Thigh, Right	23½	24½	1
,, Left	23¾	24¼	½
Calf, Right	15½	16½	1
,, Left	15½	16	½
Height	5ft. 11in.	6ft. ¼in.	1¼
Weight	13 st.	13st. 6lb	6
Lung Capacity... ...	276	320	44
Chest Expansion ...	6	7	1

Mr. Peters is a fine weight-lifter, having accomplished the splendid feat of raising 210lb from the floor to arms' length above the head, *using one hand only*. This is probably the amateur record. As he is only 23 years old there is yet plenty of time for him to far eclipse even this striking feat.

30, GUILDFORD STREET,

RUSSELL SQUARE,

W.C.,

13th March.

DEAR SIR,

It affords me *much pleasure in stating that since I commenced taking your course of instruction I have greatly increased in strength and physical development—my biceps having increased two inches, and my other muscles proportionately. I am convinced that a course of your instruction would prove beneficial to any one, whether naturally muscular or otherwise. Your system is one of such gradual progression that it cannot fail to strengthen the constitution of a person even in a delicate state of health. I shall have much pleasure in recommending your School of Physical Culture to my friends.*

Yours sincerely,

LESLIE HOOD.

EUGEN SANDOW, ESQ

LESLIE HOOD.

EBURY STREET SCHOOL.

Copy of Measurement Sheet.

Name :—L. Hood.*

Address :—30, Guildford St., W.C.

	Before Training.	After 3 months.	Increases.
Neck	15	16	1
Chest Contracted ...	$35\frac{1}{2}$	36	$\frac{1}{2}$
,, Expanded ...	$38\frac{5}{8}$	42	$3\frac{3}{8}$
Upper Arm, Right ...	$13\frac{7}{8}$	$15\frac{1}{4}$	$1\frac{3}{8}$
,, ,, Left ...	$13\frac{7}{8}$	$14\frac{3}{4}$	$\frac{7}{8}$
Fore Arm, Right ...	12	$13\frac{1}{4}$	$1\frac{1}{4}$
,, ,, Left ...	$11\frac{7}{8}$	13	$1\frac{1}{8}$
Waist	$28\frac{1}{2}$	$29\frac{1}{2}$	1
Thigh, Right	22	$22\frac{3}{4}$	$\frac{3}{4}$
,, Left	$21\frac{3}{4}$	$22\frac{1}{2}$	$\frac{3}{4}$
Calf, Right	$14\frac{3}{4}$	15	$\frac{1}{4}$
,, Left	$14\frac{1}{8}$	$14\frac{1}{2}$	$\frac{3}{8}$
Height	5ft.$7\frac{1}{4}$in.	—	—
Weight	10st.8lbs.	10st.9lbs.	1
Lung Capacity	281	—	—
Chest Expansion ...	$3\frac{1}{8}$	6	$2\frac{7}{8}$

*This pupil had been working three months before joining this school, hence the increases are not so marked as in the case of a beginner.

Roland Hastings

34, Duke Street,

St. James's, S.W.,

March 4th, 1899.

Dear Mr. Sandow,

Not often is it given to us in this life to sow our seed and gather in the full fruits of the same. Therefore it is with more than ordinary pleasure that I write this letter to say that with your system of Physical Culture this extremely satisfactory result is to be obtained.

When first I joined your school some four or five months ago I was a very fair average specimen of a young Englishman (and our national thews and sinews are by no means to be despised), but owing, in a great measure, I suppose, to my city life, I had run a little to seed, and more than once had required the aid of doctors and tonics. The advice of the former invariably ended with the same formula, " take more exercise."

I was quite ready to agree with them, as during my holidays in the country, when I was exercising in one form or another nearly the whole day, I felt quite a different man and as fit as possible.

But work in the city is a little difficult to reconcile with plenty of exercise. Some time previously Mr. Sandow had opened his school for Physical Culture, and having often admired him and his feats from afar, I resolved to go to him.

I am a business man, and from a business point of view I never did a better stroke of business in my life.

I am a mortal being, and speaking from a human point of view I never in my life came to a happier conclusion than when I resolved to become a pupil of the School of Physical Culture. I have increased in girth and weight without scarcely a superfluous ounce of flesh.

My working capabilities and staying powers are all doubled, and what before was an effort has now become a pleasure. Indigestion, torpid lassitudes, rasped nerves, and jaded appetite, are to me now unknown quantities.

With splendid appetite, long peaceful nights, and wondrous powers of vigour and vitality, I can face the world and with a deep sense of gratitude say, this is what Mr. Sandow and his system of Physical Culture have done for me.

Yours sincerely,
ROLAND HASTINGS.

P.S.—I may add I am a pupil at the ᷑. James's Street School.

St. James's Street School.

Copy of Measurement Sheet.

Name :—Roland Hastings.

Address :—Southsea House, Threadneedle St., E.C.

	Before Training.		After 3 Months.		Increases
Neck	$14\frac{1}{2}$	...	$16\frac{3}{4}$	...	$2\frac{1}{4}$
Chest Contracted ...	$34\frac{1}{2}$	...	36	...	$1\frac{1}{2}$
,, Expanded ...	$36\frac{1}{2}$	...	$43\frac{1}{4}$	...	$6\frac{3}{4}$
Upper Arm, Right ...	$11\frac{3}{4}$	...	15	...	$3\frac{1}{4}$
,, Left ...	$11\frac{5}{8}$	...	15	...	$3\frac{3}{8}$
Fore Arm, Right ...	$11\frac{7}{8}$	...	14	...	$2\frac{1}{8}$
,, Left	$11\frac{7}{8}$	...	14	...	$2\frac{1}{8}$
Waist	$29\frac{1}{4}$	...	$30\frac{3}{4}$	...	$1\frac{1}{2}$
Thigh, Right	$20\frac{1}{2}$	...	$22\frac{1}{2}$	...	2
,, Left	$20\frac{1}{2}$	...	$22\frac{1}{2}$	...	2
Calf, Right	$13\frac{1}{2}$	...	$14\frac{1}{4}$	...	$\frac{3}{4}$
,, Left	$13\frac{5}{8}$	...	$14\frac{1}{4}$	...	$\frac{5}{8}$
Height	5ft. $7\frac{1}{2}$in	...	5ft. $7\frac{1}{2}$in	...	—
Weight	10st.4lbs	...	11st. 4 lbs	...	1st.
Lung Capacity	255	...	—	...	—
Chest Expansion ...	2	...	$7\frac{1}{4}$	...	$5\frac{1}{4}$

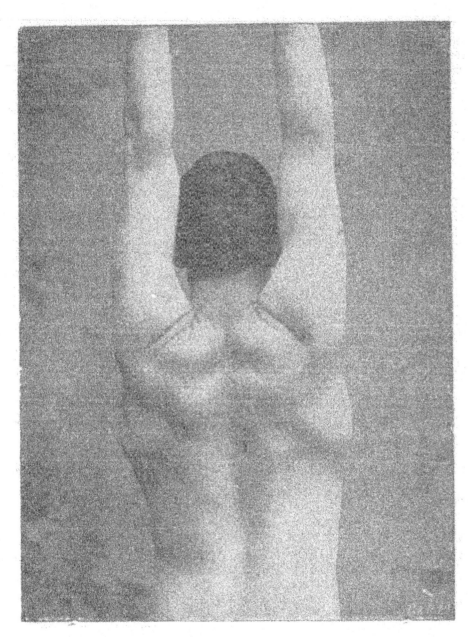

A. FOULKES.

18, St. Stephen's Road,

Bayswater, W.,

March 10th, 1899.

Dear Sir,

Your system has certainly done me a lot of good and freshened me up, although I can hardly claim to have tested it fairly, as I must plead guilty to having done none of the exercises out of the school during the three months' course that I have just concluded there.

Attending the school obviates three defects in working by yourself :—

(i.) You learn—not merely the exercises—but the way to do them.

(ii.) You get an instructor who knows his work, and keeps you at yours.

(iii.) You are stimulated by seeing others working in the same room.

The only disadvantage I can see in the system is that, if rigidly followed, you would soon be driven to patronise a fresh tailor.

I was warned not to get muscle-bound by taking the course ; I now cannot see how this can happen, unless you neglect some of the exercises entirely. I hope, at some future date, you will receive a better account of your system with regard to measurements and developments from

Yours truly,

Arthur Foulkes.

St. James's Street School.

——

Copy of Measurement Sheet.

——

Name :—A. Foulkes.

Address :—18, St. Stephen's Road, Bayswater.

	Before Training.	After 3 Months.	Increases
Neck	$14\frac{7}{8}$ ...	$17\frac{1}{4}$ ...	$2\frac{3}{8}$
Chest Contracted ...	$34\frac{1}{2}$ ...	$33\frac{5}{8}$ ...	—
,, Expanded ...	$38\frac{1}{2}$ ...	$42\frac{1}{4}$ ...	$3\frac{3}{4}$
Upper Arm, Right ...	$12\frac{1}{2}$ ...	$14\frac{1}{2}$ ...	2
,, Left ...	$11\frac{3}{4}$ ...	$14\frac{1}{4}$ ...	$2\frac{1}{2}$
Fore Arm, Right ...	$11\frac{3}{4}$ ...	13 ...	$1\frac{1}{4}$
,, Left ...	$11\frac{3}{4}$ ...	13 ...	$1\frac{1}{4}$
Waist	$30\frac{1}{4}$ ...	$31\frac{1}{2}$ ...	$1\frac{1}{4}$
Thigh, Right	$22\frac{1}{2}$ ...	24 ...	$1\frac{1}{2}$
,, Left	$22\frac{1}{2}$ ...	24 ...	$1\frac{1}{2}$
Calf, Right	$14\frac{3}{8}$ ...	$14\frac{3}{4}$ ...	$\frac{3}{8}$
,, Left	$14\frac{1}{4}$ ...	$14\frac{3}{4}$ ...	$\frac{1}{2}$
Height	6ft. ...	6ft. ...	—
Weight	12st. $1\frac{1}{2}$lb....	12st. 7 lbs. ...	$5\frac{1}{2}$
Lung Capacity	320 ...	340 ...	20
Chest Expansion ...	4 ...	$8\frac{3}{4}$ ...	$4\frac{3}{4}$

3, BURLINGTON ROAD,

BAYSWATER, W.,

March 10th, 1899.

F. A. HANSARD, ESQ.

DEAR SIR,

With regard to my opinion of Mr. Sandow's system I cannot speak too highly of it.

I commenced the three months' course when in poor health, brought about by malarial fever, but after attending Mr. Sandow's school for two months I felt better than I had ever done previously.

The increase in measurements which you have recorded is the result of two hours' conscientious work a week only.

It would be fair to mention that when only 6 lessons remained before the completion of the course, my exercises were interrupted owing to a broken collar-bone. With better luck, these increases would possibly have been greater.

I am, Sir,

Yours truly,

C. FOULKES.

C. FOULKES.

St. James's Street School.

Copy of Measurement Sheet.

Name :—C. Foulkes.

Address :—War Office, Pall Mall.

	Before Training.		After 3 Months.		Increases.
Neck	15	...	$16\frac{3}{4}$	...	$1\frac{3}{4}$
Chest Contracted ...	33	...	35	...	2
,, Expanded	38	.*1*.	43	...	5
Upper Arm, Right ..	$12\frac{5}{8}$	...	$14\frac{1}{2}$	...	$1\frac{7}{8}$
,, Left ...	$12\frac{1}{4}$	...	14	...	$1\frac{3}{4}$
Fore Arm, Right ...	$11\frac{1}{2}$	...	$13\frac{1}{2}$	...	2
,, Left ...	11	...	$13\frac{1}{3}$	...	$2\frac{1}{4}$
Waist	$30\frac{1}{2}$	...	31	...	$\frac{1}{2}$
Thigh, Right	21	...	23	...	2
,, Left	21	...	23	...	2
Calf, Right	$14\frac{1}{4}$	...	$14\frac{3}{4}$	...	$\frac{1}{2}$
,, Left	$14\frac{1}{4}$	...	$14\frac{3}{4}$	...	$\frac{1}{2}$
Height	5ft.$9\frac{1}{2}$in.	...	5ft.$9\frac{1}{2}$in.	...	—
Weight...	11st.$1\frac{1}{2}$lbs.	..	11st.4lbs.	...	$2\frac{1}{2}$
Lung Capacity	310	...	373	..	63
Chest Expansion	5	...	8	...	3

J. A. Sinclair.

YORK PLACE,

MANCHESTER,

February, 1899.

MR. E. SANDOW.

DEAR SIR,

I have much pleasure in enclosing a copy of my measurements taken at the end of last December. I am a pupil attending your Manchester School, and cannot speak too highly of your system, or the manner in which it is taught by your instructors.

Wishing you every success,

Believe me,

Yours very sincerely,

J. A. SINCLAIR.

74

OXFORD STREET SCHOOL (MANCHESTER).

COPY OF MEASUREMENT SHEET.

Name :—J. A. SINCLAIR.

Address :—York Place, Manchester.

	Before Training. Sept. 18th, 1898.		After 3 Months' Course. Dec. 28th, 1898.		In-creases.
Neck	$14\frac{1}{2}$	...	$15\frac{7}{8}$	...	$1\frac{3}{8}$
Chest Contracted* ...	$35\frac{1}{2}$	...	35	...	$\frac{1}{2}$
,, Expanded ...	37	...	$41\frac{1}{4}$	...	$4\frac{1}{4}$
Upper Arm, Right ...	14	...	$16\frac{3}{8}$	...	$2\frac{3}{4}$
,, Left ...	14	...	$16\frac{1}{4}$	...	$2\frac{1}{4}$
Fore Arm, Right ...	$11\frac{7}{8}$	...	14	...	$2\frac{1}{8}$
,, Left ...	$11\frac{5}{8}$	...	$13\frac{3}{4}$	...	$2\frac{1}{8}$
Waist...	31	...	31	...	—
Thigh, Right	$22\frac{1}{4}$	...	$24\frac{3}{4}$	...	$2\frac{1}{2}$
,, Left	$21\frac{3}{4}$	...	$24\frac{1}{4}$	...	$2\frac{1}{2}$
Calf, Right	14	...	$14\frac{7}{8}$	...	$\frac{7}{8}$
,, Left	$13\frac{3}{4}$	...	$14\frac{3}{4}$	...	1
Height	5ft. $5\frac{1}{4}$in.	...	5ft. $5\frac{1}{2}$in.	...	$\frac{1}{4}$
Weight	11st.$6\frac{1}{2}$lbs.	...	12st.0lbs.	...	$7\frac{1}{2}$
Lung Capacity	240	...	275	...	35
Chest Expansion ...	$1\frac{1}{2}$	...	$6\frac{1}{4}$	...	$4\frac{3}{4}$

*It will be noted that the size of the Chest when contracted is slightly smaller than before training ; this is not unusual, and denotes that more control has been obtained over the muscles of the chest, and consequently its walls can be drawn closer together.

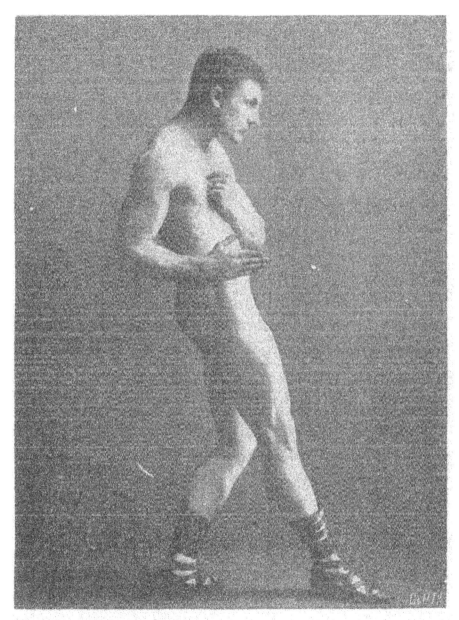

HAROLD L. BUTLER.

HIGH LAWN,

BOLTON-LE-MOORS,

March 16th, 1899.

DEAR MR. SANDOW,

After six months training as a pupil at your School of Physical Culture (Manchester), I now feel qualified to judge as to the merits of your system.

For the perfect and symmetrical development of the human form I can conceive of nothing which rivals the dumb-bell and rubber exercises as taught and practised in your gymnasia.

For the promotion of lost health, due to bodily neglect . as a cure for insomnia, and many abdominal disorders, it needs no recommendation.

Concerning my personal improvement, little need be said, sufficient to say I never felt better in my life, and recent weight-lifting tests have proved me to be possessed of nearly double my former strength.

Nor has my speed or activity suffered in the least (which so many, erroneously, consider to be the inevitable result of such training).   On the contrary, I feel as capable of doing my $10\frac{2}{5}$ *for the 100 as ever I did.*

Believe me,

Yours very truly,

HAROLD L. BUTLER

CASTELUAN,

WIMBLEDON HILL, S.W.,

March 8th, 1899.

DEAR SIR,

Having been under your system for a little over a year, I should like to add a few words in praise of your system generally. I hardly think that actual figures as to measurements and weight-lifting, give any adequate idea of the general benefits received by anyone who takes up Physical Culture thoroughly and puts his back into it.

If figures are any guide to you, however, I may quote the following, which were all taken at your School in Ebury Street.

My lung capacity has increased from 283 to 417 cubic inches, my chest expansion from $39\frac{1}{2}$ to $42\frac{1}{4}$, thigh from $20\frac{1}{2}$ to $22\frac{5}{8}$, and calf from $13\frac{7}{8}$ to $15\frac{1}{4}$.

In weight-lifting I can raise 125 lbs. from the ground with my right hand above head by means of the body-press, instead of 60 lbs. With two hands I can jerk 165 lbs. instead of 85 lbs., and I can hold out at arm's length with my right hand 45 lbs. instead of 20 lbs.

Your system has so generally benefited my **whole** *physique, however, that I consider my health has improved to an extent far beyond any actual increase in figures.*

One of the grandest benefits of Physical Culture is, to my mind, the increase of will power and general concentration, which can never be measured in any actual way, but which is bound to appear in after life, in short becomes an integral part of his character.

Yours truly,

CLAUDE BARTON.

26, GORDON MANSIONS, W.C.,

March 21st, 1899.

DEAR MR. SANDOW,

I am glad to be able to say a few words about your system of Physical Culture. I write feelingly, for I can scarcely express how grateful I am for what it has done for me. A few years back I became unpleasantly conscious that a careless disregard for my health was beginning to unfavourably affect my work before the British public. Notwithstanding the indulgence shown me by audiences in all the musical centres, I could not disguise from myself the unpalatable fact that, as a result of neglecting a cold and getting generally " run down," my singing voice was becoming seriously impaired. And so it remained until chance led me to your school of Physical Culture, and to renew the active bodily exercise which I had dropped for so long. The result was eminently satisfactory ; I was soon once more able to fulfil my public engagements with reasonable satisfaction to myself and, I trust, some pleasure to my audiences. I entirely attribute the return of my powers to the course I went through on your system.

Actors and singers do not need great muscular strength, but they do most emphatically require health, and, of course, health and reasonable development go together. No man is such a slave to his physical condition *as the actor or lyric artist. However great his talent, he cannot give expression to it if the machine be out of repair; his physical health is obviously his most valuable asset. For this reason alone I am sure that every member of my profession would be well advised to get into the way of devoting a few minutes every day to your exercises. The lyric artist especially would find his voice improve, his spirits be more exuberant, and his general vitality at a very much higher level. In addition he would in most cases discover in a very short time that his figure and limbs were so much improved that his former expenditure upon lambs-wool tights, padding, &c., would be entirely obviated.*

I am,

Yours very faithfully,

ALEC MARSH.

MARTINUS SIEVEKING.

G

PART II.

INCIDENTS OF MY PROFESSIONAL CAREER.

Sandow at the age of ten.

INCIDENTS

OF MY

PROFESSIONAL CAREER.

CHAPTER I.

MY CHILDHOOD AND BOYHOOD.

It is not necessary, as some may think, to be born strong in order to become strong. Unlike the poet, who, we are told, has to be born a poet, the strong man can make himself. As a child, I was myself exceedingly delicate. More than once, indeed, my life was despaired of. Until I was in my tenth year I scarcely knew what strength was. Then it happened that I saw it in bronze and stone. My father took me with him to Italy, and in the art galleries of Rome and Florence I was struck with admiration for the finely developed forms of the sculptured figures of the athletes of old. I remember asking my father if people were as well developed in these modern times. He pointed out that they were not, and explained that these were the figures of men who lived when might was right, when men's own arms were their weapons, and often their lives depended upon their physical strength. Moreover, they knew nothing of the modern luxuries of civilization, and, besides their training and exercise, their muscles, in the ordinary course of daily life, were always being brought prominently into play.

The memory of these muscular figures were ever present, and when we returned home to Konigsberg I wanted to become strong like them.   But though I used to try my strength and attend the gymnasium, nothing came of my desire for some years.

So until I was eighteen I remained delicate.   At that age I began to study anatomy.   It was thus I ascertained the best means of developing the body, and invented the system of giving each individual muscle a movement, and of so arranging the form of the exercises that when some muscles are brought into play others are relaxed and left without strain.

About fifteen minutes every day was the average time devoted to special exercise at this period.   It may be useful to remark here that no particular form of diet was adopted. I ate and drank in the ordinary way.   It may be said at once that I have no belief in special diet ; I have always eaten and drunk that which my fancy dictated, but I have always taken care to avoid anything in the nature of excess. There is no better guide to good living than moderation. That is a fact I am always anxious to impress upon my pupils.   Let them be moderate in all things, and they need fear no interruption in gaining strength by my system of training.

CHAPTER II.

HOW I CAME TO LONDON AND DEFEATED SAMSON.

The years of my life between eighteen and twenty-one may be passed over with the remark that they saw a steady gain of strength and some occasional performances as an amateur athlete and wrestler.

In 1889 I made the acquaintance of Aubrey Hunt, the artist, who was then at Venice. One of the most charming views in the neighbourhood was to be gained from the grounds of my villa near Ledo. Naturally Mr. Hunt wished to paint it, and it was a pleasure to be able to afford him the facility. One result of our acquaintance was that Mr. Hunt painted me in the character of a gladiator in the Coliseum at Rome. This picture, which I prize very highly, is to be seen in the reception room at my St. James' Street school. I am told that it is a very striking likeness.

It was from Mr. Hunt that I learned that Samson was offering, at the Royal Aquarium in London, £100 to the person who could perform the feats of his pupil, Cyclops, and £1,000 to anyone who could beat his own. Mr. Hunt suggested that I should accept the challenge, and it was my original intention to come to London with him. It was ultimately decided, however, that I should start without delay, and the journey to England was made on the same day that I first heard of the challenge.

Arriving in London at six o'clock in the evening, I went to Mr. Attila, a friend whom I had previously met at Brussels, to ask him to act as interpreter, for at that time I was unable to speak English. Mr. Attila not only promised his services, but gave me fresh hope by expressing his assurance that everything that Samson and his pupil could do I could accomplish easily.

We determined that the challenge should be accepted that night. With Mr. Albert Fleming to act as agent, we went at once to the Aquarium. When Samson appeared on the stage he gave the usual challenge. Apparently to his surprise, Mr. Fleming accepted it, asking him if he had the £100 at hand. Samson replied that there would be no difficulty about the money, but Mr. Fleming insisted on seeing it, and the note was accordingly produced. Samson was then asked if he had the £1,000 ready, and he promised that it would be forthcoming in the event of the defeat of his pupil.

The preliminary arrangements having been completed, and the note for £100 handed to Captain Molesworth, the manager of the Aquarium, I walked up to the stage. Seeing me in evening dress, the audience were unable to realise that I stood the slightest chance of defeating the strong man and his pupil. They even shouted to Samson not to heed me, but to get on with his performance. It seemed evident to them that I was unequal to the task that had been undertaken, and Samson himself burst out laughing when he saw me. The coolness and indifference of this first reception in London were not, perhaps, unnatural, for in evening dress there was nothing, as everyone said at the time, specially remarkable about my appearance. But when I took off my coat, and the people could see the muscular development, the tone of indifference changed immediately to surprise and curiosity. Samson and Cyclops themselves shared the general astonishment, though they did not allow their surprise to be shown for more than a moment, Samson being heard to remark, " We will beat him, anyhow."

The first feat which Cyclops performed was to lift over his head two weights of 56 lbs. each, lowering them with arms fully extended. This performance I repeated. Cyclops next took the bar bell, weighing 240 lbs., and with two hands lifted it from the ground over his head. When the audience saw that for the second time the same feat could be accomplished with ease they began to cheer; and I repeated the performance, after Cyclops, using only one hand.

All this time Samson, anxious of the issue, kept asking me in asides in French to let him know my history. As, however, he did not, or would not, speak in German, he had to remain in ignorance.

The performance proceeded, and now Cyclops took with one hand a dumb-bell weighing 210lbs., and extending it at arm's length, bent down and raised over his head with the other a second dumb-bell, of 100lbs. weight.

When I repeated this feat, it was thought that the challenge had been won, for this was the end of the performance for which it was understood it was offered. Mr. Fleming, accordingly, asked for the £100, but Samson refused, saying that the whole performance would have to be repeated and continued until one of the two competitors gave in. Nothing less would satisfy him as to which of the two was the stronger. On this point the audience disagreed, and called on him to hand over the money. Appeal was made to Captain Molesworth, who addressing the audience, promised to see fair play. He could not agree, he said, with Mr. Samson that it was fair that the performance should be continued until one of them dropped from sheer exhaustion, but he suggested that Cyclops should introduce two fresh feats, and that if I could repeat them the money should be mine without further question.

Although the audience still maintained that the challenge had been won, I expressed, through my interpreter, perfect willingness to perform not two only, but twenty more feats, should Cyclops wish to try them.

The first of the two extra feats was then taken: Cyclops lying on his back, raised a weight of 240 lbs. with two men sitting on it, and when the men jumped off he himself stood up, raising the weight with him. This performance I also repeated.

Now came the final effort. At the side of the stage stood a great stone, weighing, I should think, about 500 lbs. On this stone were secured the two 56lb. weights. Two chairs were brought, and Cyclops, standing on them, in order to get a position above the stone and its weights, raised the whole load with his middle finger some four inches above the ground.

When this performance had been repeated by me, Samson acknowledged that that part of the challenge relating to Cyclops had been won, and offered to hand over the £100.

My interpreter then explained that I had not come to London to win merely the £100; I had come for the greater sum, the £1,000, in fact, which had been offered to any person who should defeat Samson himself.

Samson, who was clearly surprised at the issue, replied that he was not prepared to meet me that night, and though the public disapproved of the postponement, it was eventually decided with Captain Molesworth that the test should be made on the following Saturday evening.

The eventful evening which was to decide the issue between us fell on the 2nd of November, 1889. Never, it was said, had the Royal Aquarium been so densely crowded. The people began to arrive as early as two o'clock in the afternoon. When I reached the building, in company with Captain Molesworth, Mr. Attila, and Mr. Fleming, twenty minutes before the hour announced for the challenge to be taken up, it was literally impossible to get through the crowd.

Here, at the very outset, was a difficulty of a new and an unexpected character. What was to be done? To try to get through the enormous throng in twenty minutes was obviously hopeless. Willing as the crowd might be to let us pass it was beyond their power to make way for us. We determined, therefore, to go to the stage door, and here a further difficulty presented itself. We could not gain admission; no one would open the heavy door. The man behind had received the strictest orders to prevent anyone from entering. In vain did Captain Molesworth implore him to let us through, explaining who we were. The man was obdurate. He said that he was very sorry, but he failed to recognise Captain Molesworth's voice, and he could not disobey explicit instructions.

All the time the precious minutes were flying, and the

hour when the challenge was to be met had actually arrived. It was, indeed, an anxious and a trying moment. We heard afterwards that when the hour of the challenge came and Samson saw that I was not there, he strutted up and down the stage, exclaiming : " Ah ! see, he does not come ! I thought he would not meet me. I will give him five minutes, nay, ten minutes more." He took out his watch, the minutes were speeding, and still Samson stood alone.

Meanwhile, resolved not to be baffled by this absurd mischance, it was determined that, as fair words would not open the door, strength should smash it open. A blow well directed, and the door was burst from its hinges. The man inside was slightly injured by this rough method, but a ten pound note served to solace his feelings, and to heal his wounds. And we—well, we just managed to save the challenge by the space of half-a-minute.

The Marquis of Queensberry and Lord de Clifford were appointed judges, and they examined closely all the bars, bells, weights, and chains that were to be used in the performance. Samson first desired that I should follow him in some juggling feat with a water bottle, but the judges decided that this was not in the order of the performance. Only such tests of actual strength as Samson was in the habit of displaying could now be allowed. Samson, abiding by this decision, took a large iron bar and bent it over his calf, his arms, and his neck, just as, in a similar way, by striking it on the muscles of the arm, one may bend a poker. The thing is little more than a trick. Of course, muscle is essential to its successful performance ; for if you have no muscle you will hit the bone, with the danger of breaking it. Such a performance, although there is a certain knack in doing it gracefully, and with ease, was not difficult to follow.

Samson next took a wire cable, winding it round his chest, under his arms, and then breaking it. This feat, which is performed by inflating the lungs and at the same time contracting the muscles of the chest, I was also able to repeat.

By the third item in the display it seemed that Samson

desired to leave the issue of the challenge in doubt, for it consisted in snapping a chain which encircled his arm. This armlet, which fitted Samson well enough, was too small for me. Fortunately I was prepared for the emergency. I had ascertained where the chain was bought, and had got the same firm to make me an armlet of exactly the same strength, of a size suitable to my larger development. When I produced it, Samson at first refused to be satisfied that it would be a fair test, but a representative of the firm who made it stood up in the auditorium and assured the public that it was of the same strength as that of the chain made for Samson. The judges examined it, together with the paper which testified to the equality of strength, and decided that the test would be perfectly fair and that the performance was to continue. I placed the chain on my arm and broke it.

Samson was still dissatisfied, and I made the offer that if either he or his pupil, Cyclops, could repeat my performance with a dumb-bell which I had at hand, we would declare the result a draw, and he could keep his £1,000. The dumb-bell, which was then brought on to the stage, weighed 280lbs. With one hand I lifted it up, then laid down, and finally stood up with it. After that feat I fastened some chains round my arms, then took a dumb-bell weighing 220lbs., raised it to my chest and burst the chains before releasing it.

"I have had enough of this," now exclaimed Samson. "It's all humbug, I don't call this fair play at all."

The judges, however, were sufficiently satisfied, and Mr. Fleming asked for the £1,000. The reply was that it should be paid in the morning, but it remains to be added that I never received that £1,000. It was stated that Samson had taken his money away, and in the end I agreed to accept £350 from the management of the Aquarium in settlement of the challenge.

When we left the Aquarium after the contest the great crowd followed us cheering, and the four-wheeled cab into which we got, was lifted up by these enthusiasts. The crowd cheered us all the way to my rooms in Leicester-square; newspaper men poured in to interview me; and though I had then no intention of giving performances in public, I was induced to accept one of numerous offers, of £150 a week, made by a syndicate of the members of the Lyric Club, and I commenced an engagement at the Alhambra, giving Mr. Attila £30 a week to assist me.

I spent three months at the Alhambra, and three months in the provinces, and entered into engagements for some years to come.

The reader will probably ask if special means were adopted during this and succeeding engagements to maintain my strength. The answer is very simple: The performance itself provides the necessary amount of daily training. I eat, drink, smoke, and sleep quite in the ordinary way, taking care to observe in all things that guiding rule of moderation to which reference is made in the preceding chapter. I only practice, in order that grace and perfection may be attained, when some new feat is introduced. Personally it may be added, I find that the best time for a performance is about three hours after a meal.

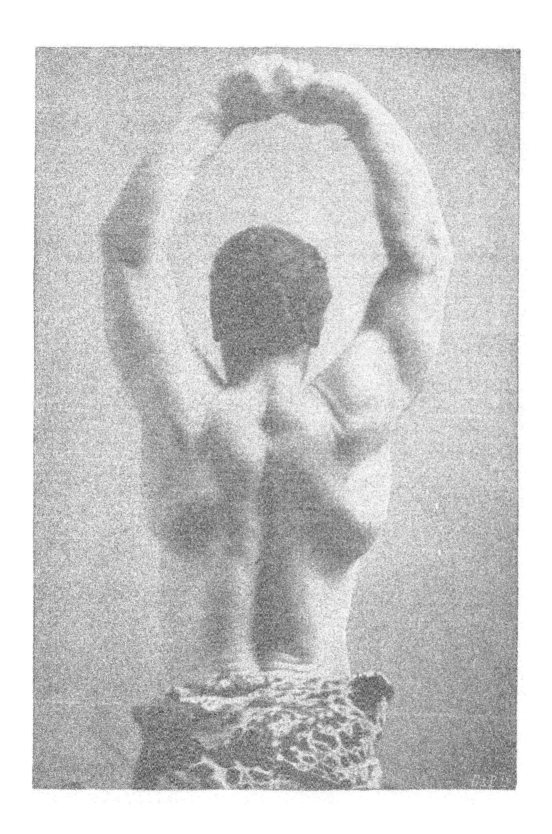

CHAPTER III.

I MEET GOLIATH.

At the end of my first engagement in London and the provinces, I went to Germany for a holiday. Driving out one day at Aachen, I met a veritable giant. He was a quarryman, and he was engaged in loading stones. So huge and extraordinary was his appearance that my horse positively shied at him.

Imagine, if you can, this tremendous fellow : his head as huge and grotesque as that of any pantomime mask, with a nose the size of an ordinary fist. As for his own fist, it would have made more than three of mine, and when a five-shilling piece was placed beneath the ball of his finger, believe me, it was impossible to see it. So large were his boots that not only could I get both my feet into one, but I could turn entirely round inside. And yet, strangely enough, despite his immense limbs and body, he was not an extraordinarily tall man. A little more than six feet; six feet two-and-a-half inches, in fact, was his height. His chest measurement was about eighty inches and his weight 400lbs. He was not a fat man in proportion to his size. Quite the contrary. He was bony and muscular.

The thought occurred to me as soon as I saw him that to give him a part in a performance as a modern Goliath would be, from a popular point of view, eminently attractive. I asked him what wages he was earning. " Five marks a day," he replied. It appeared that he was given nearly double the pay of an ordinary labourer because he could lift heavier weights and load the carts more quickly. I told him that if he liked to accept an engagement with me I would give him twenty marks a day, whether he worked or not. A

German mark, as everyone knows, is equivalent to an English shilling. The giant quarryman could scarcely credit such good fortune, and eventually it was agreed that he should come to my house to talk the proposal over, and have his strength tested. When he came it was found that he could do nothing more than lift heavy weights from the floor. He had never put himself into training, and his exceptional proportions, which, under different circumstances, might have been turned to good account, were of no special use to him. However, it was settled that he should come with me, and I brought him to England.

Well do I remember our arrival at Charing Cross. The huge size of Goliath, whose real name, by the way, was Karl Westphal, attracted the most pronounced attention. It was impossible to think of taking a cab, for no cab would have held him, even if he had been able to get inside it. There was, therefore, nothing for it but to walk to my chambers, which were then in Rupert-street, Piccadilly. Thousands of people followed us the whole way, and Rupert-street was blocked. A giant, when you have got him, is rather like a white elephant. He is a rare creature, but it is difficult to know what to do with him. It would have been clearly unwise to let him go into the streets, and accordingly he had to be kept indoors. For seven or eight weeks I tried to train him, but he proved an idle fellow, and it became evident that nothing much could be done with him.

I had an engagement at that time at the Royal Music Hall, and a performance was arranged in which Goliath had to surprise me, lumbering after me across the stage, and trying to hold me in his grip.

We wrestled together, and it was his business to make himself the victor. Then, in order to finish me, he took a cannon, weighing 400lbs., and placing it on his broad shoulders, prepared to fire. In a moment or so I returned with the clubs. It was now the turn of the giant to show alarm, and gradually he had to retire, with the cannon still on his back, into a frame of refuge. I at once climbed to the top, and getting into a position above my antagonist, I lifted him, his refuge, and his cannon, with one finger, a few inches off the ground. During this part of the performance we fired the cannon, and the whole display was brought to a conclusion by placing my arm through a leathern belt which girt his waist, and carrying him at arm's length off the stage.

What became of him after he left me I never heard. The last report was that he had carried off his own landlady, and that the two had started some sort of show together.

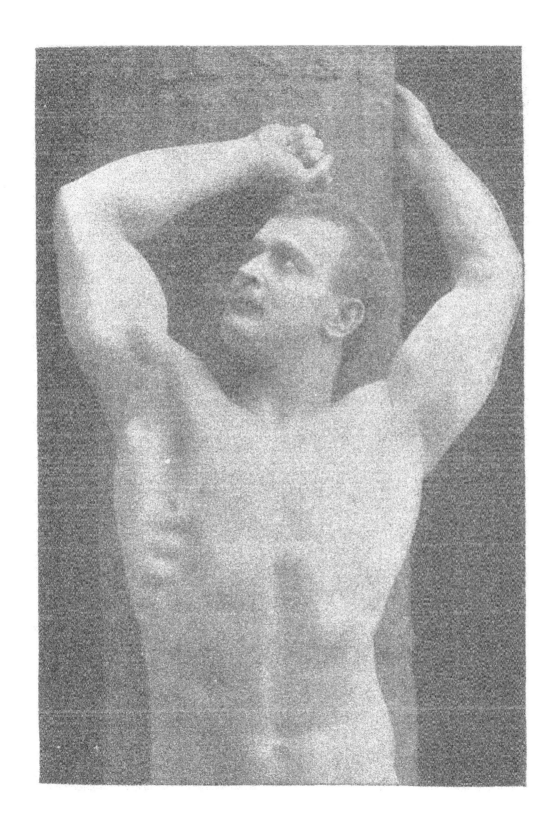

CHAPTER IV.

A PRESENTATION UNDER CURIOUS CIRCUMSTANCES.

After my engagement at the Royal came a holiday in Paris. It was there I met a very dear school friend, whom I had not seen since I was about ten years of age. My friend's father was at this time German Consul at Paris. The incident which followed our meeting will be better explained by prefacing the story with the statement that as boys we were great billiard players. We were continually playing at each other's houses, and, though we were such mere lads, we could even beat our fathers at the game. Nothing, therefore, was more natural than that, when we met, my friend should ask me if I was still a good player. As a matter of fact I was not in practice, but that did not deter us from deciding to try our skill. So we went to a room which he selected, and started a game. He did not know then that I had made my strength a profession; he was rather under the impression that I had followed my father's desire and studied medicine. However, the game began, and, as we talked a good deal over old times and spoke in German and played rather slowly, I suppose we unconsciously annoyed a party of Frenchmen. At any rate they made unfriendly remarks, and before we had finished our game they marked on the slate that they had engaged the table. Wishing to play again, we were not disposed to give it up to people whose manner was obviously offensive. As our right to continue was disputed, the attendant was called, and it was pointed out that, according to the regulations of the establishment,

we were perfectly within our rights in playing a second
game. So we played on, and whilst we were joking and
laughing about old times they, it seems, thought we were
making fun of their discomfiture.

When the game was finished we ordered two steaks,
which were served at a table behind the players.   We were
still laughing over old times when one of the party came up,
saying angrily, "I've had enough of your laughter ; if you
don't stop be sure I'll make you."

I told him that I was very sorry that my mood offended
him, and if I could not laugh at our own personal jokes
I should be sorrier still.   It was added that I did not wish
to interfere with him, and it was suggested also that he
should attend to his own game and leave us alone.

It was evident that he wished to pick a quarrel.   Nor
would hot words suffice him.   Vowing that he must give
me something to remember him by, he struck me across the
face.   Beneath this fresh insult I tried to remain quite calm,
telling my assailant that it would be certainly better for
him to take himself off and leave me alone.   But at such
times, when the temper is quick, good advice is not heeded ;
moreover, he probably thought he had to deal with some
one of poor spirit.

Whatever may have been in his mind the facts are plain :
finding that I took one blow calmly he struck me another
and called me coward.   My friend, who had hitherto kept
quiet, now attempted to interfere, but I held him down,
nearly wrenching his wrist round.   The force which was
exerted must have given him an idea of the strength that
was ready to be used if it were needed, for looking first at
his wrist and then at me, he exclaimed in English, " Why
don't you knock the fellow down ?"

"So you speak English," said the Frenchman, " Why
don't you get up and fight me?" With these words he
struck me fiercely on the nose.   The blood streamed down my
clothes, which were spoilt besides by the gravy that was
splashed on them in the disturbance from the dishes.   My
appearance must have been deplorable, and as I was that
morning wearing a new suit, I lost my patience with the man.
I walked slowly towards him, and with a quick grip of

his neck and knees, I picked him up, knocked his head and knees together, and banged him down in the centre of the table. The table broke through, and he fell to the ground. You can imagine, I daresay, the scene of wreckage and consternation—the smashed table, the man dazed, lying in a heap on the floor, his friends around him open-mouthed with amazement. In the midst of this scene I sat down with my friend and smoked a cigar.

A gendarme was fetched. He entered the room and wanted to arrest me. The proprietor caught hold of him, saying, "Be careful, he is an awful man, he will kill you. You must have some assistance." Four more gendarmes were summoned, and, refusing to take me in a cab, they marched me along to the police station. Some of the friends of the man who was hurt accompanied us and explained to the authorities that the regrettable affair was not my fault. They were sorry at what had happened, and I was liberated on bail.

Meanwhile they took their injured comrade to the hospital. He was still unconscious, and in that condition he remained a day and a half. Being sincerely sorry for the injury I had caused, I called at the hospital and asked to see him, but he refused.

As soon as he recovered, which was not for some weeks, I left Paris to return to London to fulfil an engagement at the Tivoli.

One night, whilst I was performing there, the porter brought me a message asking if I would step up to see a gentleman and a party of friends in a private box. When I went up I seemed to recognise the face of the person who wished to see me, but I could not recall where I had seen it before. The party invited me to take wine with them, and nothing would satisfy them but my consent to be their guest at supper.

When we reached the hotel, my host said : " I perceive, Mr. Sandow, you have only pretended that you know me. You do not really recall my identity."

It had to be confessed that he was right.

" If you really knew me," he proceeded, " you would probably not speak to me.

"Why not?" I asked. "I speak to you because I seem to like you, surely that is sufficient."

"We will see," he added; "I have come a long way to see you. I have come from Paris. I am an amateur in your own line, performing feats of strength myself. Of all my friends I have the reputation of being the strongest. Having read of your performances in the French and English papers, I was determined to come to London to see you. I saw the whole programme at the Tivoli to-night, waiting impatiently for your display. When you stepped on to the stage I nearly dropped to the ground."

"Why"! I asked, growing curious.

Tears stood in his eyes, as he exclaimed earnestly, "Will you promise to forgive me, promise me that or I cannot tell you."

I told him that I did not know what I had to forgive, but at any rate I promised to forgive him in advance.

"Well," he went on, "if I had known you were Mr. Sandow I would never have struck you that blow in Paris;" and then in enthusiastic French fashion he clung hold of me and kissed me on the cheek—on the cheek that he had previously smacked—before all the people.

Of course, why had I been so blind? This was my assailant of the French billiard room. All, however, was now forgiven and forgotten, and as a token of our good understanding he presented me with a handsome gold watch. To-day we are the greatest friends, and, whenever I go to Paris, I stay with him. He is a French Count, but for obvious reasons, not the least being that he is my friend, despite the hard knocks which came of our first meeting, it would not be fair to disclose his name.

CHAPTER V.

THE LIVING WEIGHTS.

About this time there were many strong men.   Each hall in London could boast of at least one.   It was also a great weight lifting period.   When I lifted my heaviest bell, 280lbs., the other strong men put out a placard stating that they were lifting 300lbs.   By the time I had practised sufficiently to raise the weights I was lifting from 280lbs. to 300lbs., they came out with the statement that they were lifting 320lbs., and so their little game went on.

For my part I was determined to introduce a novelty. Henceforth, there should be actually living weights.   I started, therefore, at the Tivoli with a new display, lifting a horse at arm's length above my head, and marching with it to musical accompaniment.

This was followed by a display with human dumb-bells. Taking a long bar with a large ball at each end, I placed in each ball a man, and I raised bar, balls, and men, slowly over the head.   After putting them down the balls opened and the men rolled out.   This performance I accomplished in order to equal the feat of lifting 300lbs. dead weight.

Further, I lifted, and supported on my chest, a grand pianoforte, with an orchestra of eight performers on top of the instrument.

There was still a fourth feat which I performed, knowing that no one could equal it, and that was to turn a somersault whilst holding a weight of 56lbs. in each hand.

These performances I repeated in the provinces.   During this tour I had the pleasure of visiting not only many of the chief cities of England, but also Edinburgh and Glasgow.

Who can fail to be deeply impressed by the grandeur and magnificence of the scenery of Scotland? Certainly I was not proof against it. Never have I visited a more beautiful city than Edinburgh, and the Scottish people themselves I found exceedingly kind and agreeable. Since then, I have been to Ireland, and can testify that its people are as frank, generous, and warm-hearted, as they are always represented to be. Certainly, some of the happiest days of my life were those spent in the Emerald Isle.

At the end of my first provincial tour I returned to London to fulfil an engagement at the Palace Theatre. Here I introduced another novelty. In place of the orchestra I held three horses on my chest. These animals stood on a plank, one at each side and the third in the centre, holding the balance in a game of see-saw. Included in this performance was the feat in which a Horse Guardsman on his horse rode over me, thus completing at that time the chapter of living weights.

------> <------

I

CHAPTER VI.

ON THE "ELBE": BOUND FOR NEW YORK.

We come now to the year of the Chicago Exhibition, when I entered into a contract for an engagement in America, with Messrs. Abbey, Scheffel, and Grau.

An old friend and famous pianist, Martinus Sieveking, whom I knew years before in Belgium and Holland, accompanied me to the New World. Sieveking was a brilliant artist, but as a man he was exceedingly weak and delicate. He had no powers of endurance, and it was difficult for him to remain at the piano long at a time.

" If I had only your strength," he used to say, " I think I might become almost the greatest player in the world."

I suggested that he should come with me as my guest to America, guaranteeing that in nine months or a year, under my personal supervision and training, he would grow so strong that his best friends would scarcely recognise him.

Agreeing to come, he travelled with me all through America. The result of my system and supervision was that his strength grew marvellously. Within the year, weak as he was at the start, he became the strongest of all my pupils, and the most redoubtable amateur I have ever met. The portrait, which is printed on an earlier page will speak for itself when you remember that a year before it was taken the sitter had a gaunt, slim, delicate figure, with narrow chest, sloping shoulders, and no muscles worth speaking about.

But I am going ahead too fast. Let us revert for a moment to our departure from England. We sailed on the Elbe, the vessel that was afterwards wrecked. There was a good deal

I 2

of bustle in getting on board, and some curiosity, I suppose, amongst the passengers, when they saw the sailors straining beneath the weight of my luggage and apparatus, and got to know that a strong man was to sail with them. With the captain and the first engineer I became very friendly giving them, during the voyage, lessons in my system.

Somehow I used to feel that the ship we were on was a doomed vessel. I am not ordinarily superstitious, and it is not necessary to attempt to account for the feeling, but do what I would I could not shake off the dread impression that one day that ship would go down. I became so friendly with the engineer, whom I used to visit in his own cabin, that I advised him to give up his appointment and go to sea no more.

Some time after that, whilst I was in America, the world was startled by the news of the Elbe's disaster. My friend, the engineer, was amongst the few who were saved. He wrote me a letter telling me of the tidings. This letter touched me very deeply, and, seeing that it contains a story of singular bravery, it may not be inappropriate if I introduce here so much of it as I remember.

Having commented on the strange fulfilment of my prediction, he described how, when the boat was going down, the captain lashed himself to the bridge, saying he would never leave his ship. From the engineer's boat they called to him to come on, but he would not stir. Then they sent back the pilot, but still to no purpose. By the faint glimmer of a lantern he pencilled a note which he asked might be sent, if the bearer should be saved, with his heart's love to his dear wife and children. For the last time the pilot left the ship, and as the boat bore away from its now fast sinking sides the captain from the bridge, immovable from the post of duty, waved his long farewell.

CHAPTER VII.

MY FIRST HOUR IN AMERICA.

First experiences are occasionally curious. You shall hear one of mine.

Although the day we reached New York was the hottest that had ever been known in that great country of wonderful records, no heat, however extreme, could detract from the glories of New York Harbour, certainly the finest harbour I have ever seen. Numerous people, including, of course, the ubiquitous newspaper men, came on board to welcome me, bands were playing, and there was a gay and busy time generally.

Having landed, I entered a cab. Everyone, I suppose, has a vivid recollection of his first cab in America. The independence of the American cab-driver is sublime. It is something too great for words. You can only draw a long breath—and admire it. The particular journey which I was undertaking would have been in England something considerably less than a shilling fare. Hoping to be generous I proffered the driver an equivalent in English money to two shillings. To my surprise he said, " I guess, Colonel, that's for myself; your fare is four dollars "—just eight times as much as I had offered. Of course, I could not argue with the man. He knew better than I, and there was nothing for it but to pay promptly what he demanded. Moreover, in America, it must be remembered, they charge, not for the drive, but for the cab.

Mr. Abbey, who met me on the boat, accompanied me to the hotel at which I was to stay. At the office his attention was called away for a moment, and I was left to the tender mercies of the bell boy, a nigger, who was asked to show me the rooms.

"Come along, sir," the boy drawled. And along I went, making my first acquaintance with an American elevator, in which we were shot up heavenwards.

"How high are we?" I asked, as we got out.

"Oh, this is the sixteenth floor," replied the boy, in an off-hand manner, "you can see if you look down." I did look down. By Jove, the depth down that staircase was tremendous.

Having selected my apartments, the boy coolly stood beside me in my own room rolling a cigarette and lighting it in my presence. This action seemed a little impudent, but it was nothing to that which was to come. Remarking that I desired to wash, I also asked the boy if he would clean my boots.

"Clean your boots?" he exclaimed, in blank astonishment, "we don't do that in America, we (speaking of course for himself and the niggers like him) don't clean boots here."

"Who then," I asked, "does clean them?"

"Oh, you must go down stairs for that." And with these words he reclined on my sofa, rolled another cigarette, and calmly smiled at me.

This was really too much for white flesh and blood to bear. I said to him sharply, "Look here, young man; I may be a stranger in this country and ignorant of some of its ways, but I know enough of Americans to be quite sure that it is not right for you to conduct yourself in this way. If you don't promptly clear off I will report you?"

But the boy was not easily to be moved. Instead of taking himself off he squared up and wanted to fight me. So I just took hold of that boy, and testing his jacket and trousers to be sure that they would bear the strain, I swung him over the sixteenth floor staircase. And there for a few moments I held him, just to give him a view of the depth, which was so tremendous.

My word, didn't that boy shout and scream! I assured him that he was quite safe in my hand so long as it was closed, but if he ever attempted his impertinences again I would bring him to the same spot and open it. And

I reminded him that a drop through sixteen floors would not be good even for nigger boys who smoked cigarettes in private rooms and affected to be indignant at the suggestion that they should clean a visitor's boots.

The boy's cries drew a small crowd, including Martinus Sieveking and the manager of the hotel. The manager fully agreed with the warning I gave the boy, and was profuse in his apologies, saying that such conduct from a bell boy was unprecedented.

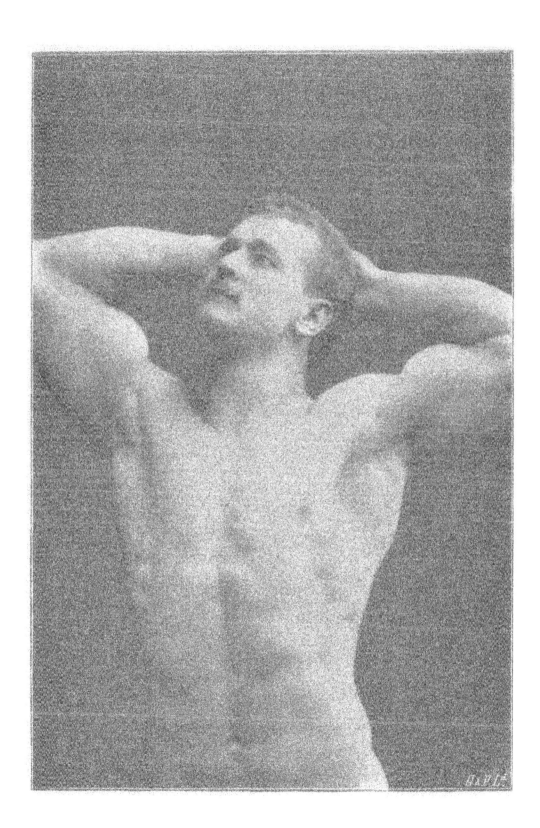

CHAPTER VIII.

INCIDENTS OF THE AMERICAN TOUR.

A fortnight after my arrival in New York I commenced an engagement at the Casino, and after each performance, whilst I was still stripped to the waist, I gave lectures on anatomy and my system of physical culture in my dressing-room. These lectures were attended by many of the most notable people in America, the crowded audiences including several ladies. I demonstrated how each feat was accomplished, and let the people feel for themselves my muscles, to prove that whilst, when they were relaxed they were as soft as butter, when contracted they were as hard as steel.

I repeated at the Casino the performances that I had been giving at the Palace Theatre in London. As my engagement lengthened I grew better acquainted with the American people, whom, let it frankly be admitted, I liked immensely. They are wonderfully nice fellows, these Americans. The only fault that is to be found with them is the too generous length to which their hospitality is liable to go in the direction of cock-tails. They like to give you a bath of cock-tails, and if a bath should not suffice, they would think nothing of making a river for you. For a moderate drinker like myself, their generosity is a little embarrassing, but as the point was emphasised that I could never have the assurance to say that I had been to America without tasting a cock-tail, I at last yielded to their persuasions, and, judging from the samples of Manhattan, Martini, and Oyster, which I tried, I am bound to confess that these drinks are exceedingly nice, and that there is little to beat them. Another striking feature of life in America is to be found in the trotting horses. They are simply marvellous creatures, moving with the ease and almost with the speed of a railway engine.

From New York I went to Boston, where my system of physical training became very fashionable ; and after the Boston visit came Chicago, Mr. Sieveking always accompanying me.

When I arrived at Chicago I went to the Trocadero, where I was to appear, and inquired for the manager. A tall slim fellow made his appearance in answer to the inquiry, and for some minutes a game of cross purposes ensued. For whilst I was not sure whether he really was the manager, he doubted whether I was the strong man whom he expected. At last, however, I ascertained that he was Mr. Ziegfeld, or at least Mr. Ziegfeld's son, and he was assured that I was Sandow. He showed me round the theatre, which was a tremendous place, with accommodation for fully six thousand people. It had been originally an armoury, and was used more for concerts than variety entertainments. Mr. Ziegfeld had taken it because his other theatre, two days before the opening of the exhibition, was burned down. At the time of my arrival it was proving too big, but, as good luck would have it, such was the popularity of my performances, the building, despite its huge size, was filled nightly.

In the exhibition grounds one morning shortly after my arrival, Mr. Ziegfeld suggested that I should drive round in one of the hand wagons.

"My dear fellow," I said, "it would never do for a strong man to be pushed round like that, what would the people say ? "

"Oh, they don't know you yet," replied Mr. Ziegfeld, " you get in and try it."

It was no use for me to chaff him by saying that these wagons were more suitable for idle fellows of his slim proportions, for inside he would have me get. Who of all people in the world should come to push me round but an unfortunate hunchback ! The result was that next morning the papers came out with illustrations of the ludicrous scene, with the heading " The strong man too strong to walk."

At the termination of the World's Fair, Mr. Ziegfeld proposed that I should prolong my tour. I accepted his suggestion, engaged him as my manager, and he booked a tour for me, including all the principal cities. Throughout this tour I offered at each performance ten thousand dollars to any person who could duplicate my feats of strength or even do anything that could be said reasonably to approach them.

At St. Louis, one of the greatest beer brewing districts in the world, the challenge, I was informed, was to be accepted. The youth who was prepared to meet me, explained that he was somewhat too stiff to accomplish all my feats, and I accordingly promised that if he could repeat one of them, that was to lift with one hand over his head my heaviest dumb-bell weighing 300lbs., I would consent to give him the money.

When the time came for him to take up the challenge, he grew alarmed at the prospect. In answer to my manager's announcement from the stage that we were ready for him, and that the money had been duly deposited, he stood up in the auditorium to remark that the challenge was made only as an advertisement, he did not believe in it, and he refused to come to the stage. With these words he rushed out of the building. His friends, who had a good deal of faith in his physical powers, rushed after him, and succeeded in bringing him back. In order further to encourage his droop-ing spirits my manager offered him the ten thousand dollars if he would lift the weight over his head with both hands. But still he did not like to attempt the task he had before rashly undertaken. We then reduced the conditions still further, promising that if he would lift the weight with two hands even as high as his shoulders we would still give him the money. His friends now chaffed and now rallied him, and at last he put his strength to the test ; but lo, this vaunted strong man was a very weak man, for so far from being able to raise the weight to his shoulders, he succeeded scarcely in moving it from the ground

K

CHAPTER IX.

MY LION FIGHT IN SAN FRANCISCO.

Perhaps the greatest, certainly the most thrilling, of all my experiences is that which I am about to relate. It is the story of my lion fight in San Francisco.

I was performing in that western city at the time of the mid-winter fair, which followed the Chicago Exhibition. In connection with this fair Colonel Bone was exhibiting a great menagerie. One day he advertised a fight to the death between a lion and a bear. A tremendous tent, with accommodation for twenty thousand people, was erected for the occasion. Thousands and thousands of persons had bought tickets, when the police issued an order forbidding the performance, and the proposed spectacle had to be abandoned.

The thought occurred to me that I should take the bear's place, and measure my strength against the king of the forests. Of course there is always between the unarmed man and the beast this disadvantage, that the beast has natural weapons in his teeth and claws, whilst a man has nothing to help him in the fight. This lion, moreover, was a particularly furious animal. Only a week before he made a meal of his keeper. I have met many lions in various places, and this beast was certainly the largest and finest of them all. I was fully prepared to meet him as he was, provided I could have an equivalent for his claws in a short dagger or some similar weapon ; but the law in America, as in England, is rightly very stern against cruelty to animals, and the dagger, of course, could not be allowed. If I desired to meet the beast the only way was to fight him as I would box a man, completely unarmed. As there is no law to prevent cruelty to men, there was no objection to this method, though Colonel Bone, as well as my own friends, insisted that if there was to be a fight it must be a struggle between brute strength and human strength. In short, mittens would have to be placed on the lion's feet to prevent him from tearing me to pieces with his claws, and a muzzle would have to be placed over his head. Even with these precautions I was advised not to proceed with the contest. "With his strength," said Colonel Bone, "he'll knock your head off." But, personally, I had no fear, I was only anxious for the contest to begin. The engagement was accordingly made, and "A lion fight with Sandow" was boldly advertised. The announcement sent a thrill through the cities for hundreds of miles around, and in order fully to be equipped for a performance which would be bound to attract thousands and thousands of people, I decided to rehearse my fight with the lion beforehand.

Accordingly, preparations were made, and with much difficulty the lion was mittened and muzzled. It took several men with lassos and chains some hours to perform this operation, for not only had they to guard against the animal's overpowering strength, but they had to proceed cautiously in order not to injure him. A great cage, measuring seventy feet across, was brought round, and into it Colonel Bone, one of the most experienced of lion tamers, let the animal enter. Few people were present, but amongst them was my manager, that tall, slim, great, little Ziegfeld, with a face white as snow. There is no doubt that Mr. Ziegfeld and the small company felt the position acutely, for though personally I had confidence in myself—and confidence of victory is always half a battle won—yet those around were by no means sure of the issue, and there was some fear that my first fight with a lion might be my last.

However, my purpose being fixed, I entered the cage, unarmed and stripped to the waist. The lion, with fury in his eyes, crouched down ready to spring. Having read a good deal of the methods of the lion I was not unprepared for this form of attack. As he made his last strain for a tremendous leap I stepped sharply to the side and he missed his mark. Turning quickly before he had time fully to recover, I caught him round the throat with my left arm, and round the middle with my right. By this means, though his weight was 530lbs., I lifted him as high as my shoulder, gave him a good hug to assure him that it was necessary to respect me, and tossed him on to the floor.

Thus outdone at his first attempt, the lion roared with rage. Rushing fiercely towards me he raised his huge paw to strike a heavy blow at my head. For the moment, feeling the swish of the lion's paw as it passed my face, I really thought that Colonel Bone's remark that he would knock my head off would prove true. Luckily I dodged my head just in time, and got a good grip round the lion's body, with my chest touching his and his feet over my shoulders. Now came the tussle ; the more I hugged him the more he scratched and tore, and, though his feet were mittened, he tore through my tights and parts of my skin. But I had got him as in a vice, and his efforts to get away were fruitless. Choosing an opportune moment, I flung him off me, Colonel Bone and my manager shouting to me to come out of the cage, as I had done enough, and the lion's rage was unbounded.

I was determined, however, before I left to try just one other feat. Moving away from the lion, I stood with my back towards him, thus inviting him to jump on me. I had not to wait many moments. He sprang right on my back. Throwing up my arms I gripped his head, then caught him firmly by the neck, and in one motion, shot him clean over my own head to the ground before me. Colonel Bone rushed into the cage, snapping two revolvers to keep the lion off, and I came out, my legs torn, my neck bleeding, and with scratches all over my body ; but I felt that I had mastered that lion, and that I should have little difficulty in mastering him again at the performance that was to be given next day in public.

When the hour for the fight came, the huge tent which held twenty thousand people was literally packed in every part. The cage with the lion was outside, and whilst he was being mittened and muzzled he became so furious that he broke two iron chains that bound him, and got loose. The people shrieked, the very men who a moment before had been boasting of their bravery, were the first to fly, and there was a general stampede. But the moment the lion saw my eyes fixed fearlessly and firmly on him he seemed paralysed. Colonel Bone came up and pulled out his revolver, telling me not to take my eyes off him, as I had him in my power. Whilst we both remained motionless, the cage was brought near his head, and by a dexterous movement I had him over on his back, and once more he was a prisoner. The keepers tried again to mitten him, and after a great struggle they succeeded.

Then came the scene in the arena. The lion appeared first, and as I entered the whole place shook with cheers and applause. Through the whole of that vast assembly ran a thrill of great excitement, and photographers were there ready to take instantaneous pictures of the various positions of the fight with the lion. But no sooner did I enter the cage than the animal cowered down. He knew that I was his master: and he refused to fight. Feeling that the audience would be sadly disappointed, I tried to goad him on, but nothing would move him. Most beasts are cowards at heart, and this lion having met his match at the rehearsal, refused to budge.

At last I caught hold of his tail and twisted it. This was the only thing that moved him. As he made a bound towards me I dodged, swung round and picked him up, and then tossed him down. The fight lasted scarcely two minutes. The lion, recognising that my strength was too much for him, would fight no more. Though I lifted him up and walked round the arena with him on my shoulders he remained as firm as a rock and as quiet as a lamb. The fierce fight at the rehearsal had subdued his courage. He was clearly conquered. I was afraid that my audience would be disappointed with the comparative tameness of the proceedings, but, on the contrary, everyone seemed thoroughly satisfied, and " the lion fight with Sandow " was long the talk of the day in San Francisco.

CHAPTER X.

FURTHER INCIDENTS OF THE TOUR.

At the end of my engagement in San Francisco I organised my own company for a holiday tour in California. What a lovely country is that; a country of perpetual summer and blue sky, of bright flowers and delicious breezes. Well do I remember our arrival in Los Angelos. Thousands and thousands of people came to meet our coach, the children smothering us with roses as though it were some battle of flowers.

But, of course, there were rough journeys in America as well as pleasant ones. On the way to Omaha, for example, we had an experience of the wilds. At the small villages at which the train stopped it seemed to be the custom to adjourn for the fifteen or twenty minutes to the gambling dens that adjoin the stations. Gambling has never had any attraction for me personally, but " In Rome one does as Rome does ; " and so in America. Accordingly, we visited one of these gambling houses. There is no question about the gambling. You play with dice. Everything is conducted at lightning speed, and before you know where you are high stakes have been lost or won—usually, it may be said, they are lost. In our case we started, in the few minutes at our disposal, by winning a good deal. Then we lost, and we left that place with our pockets practically empty. I had lost three hundred dollars, another lost four hundred, and a third eight hundred.

During the next part of the journey we heard that there was another gambling house at the station at which we should stop on our way. It was in connection, we understood, with that at which we had just lost our money, and no doubt the manager would be informed by telegram of the easy manner in which we had been duped, in order to be prepared for our arrival. But we were determined to be even with those gambling house keepers. We agreed at the start not to risk more than five dollars, and if we won we would depart with our winnings before the luck, as in the last case, set in against us. For once expectations were realised. Precisely the same thing happened. At the beginning we had all the luck ; we not only recovered what we had previously lost, but each of us had a few hundred dollars to the good. Then of a sudden our luck began to turn. That was the signal. There was six or seven minutes to spare before the train started, and the manager and his friends said " You have lots of time, gentlemen, they will tell you when the train's ready." Much to their astonishment, however, we insisted on leaving, and as we walked out with our pockets fairly full the faces of those men were a study. I think on this occasion we had turned the tables successfully.

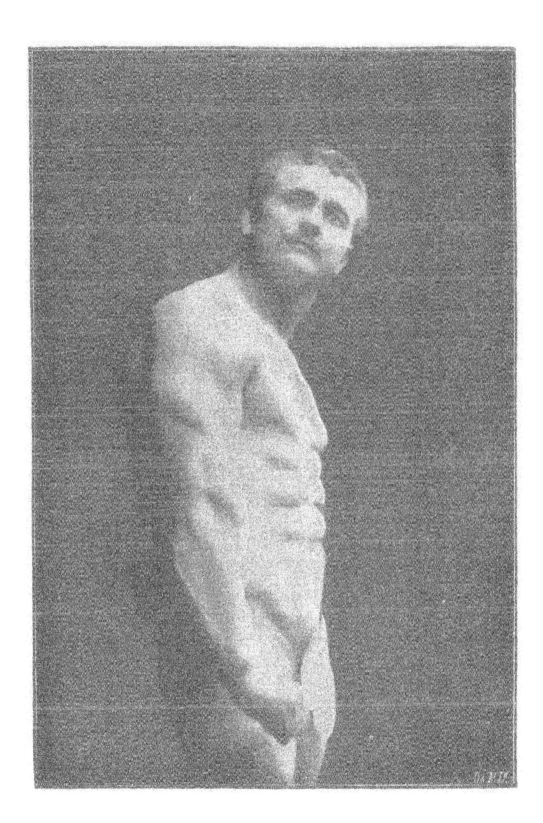

CHAPTER XI.

MY DOG SULTAN. END OF THE TOUR.

At this stage of the tour I will introduce, with the reader's permission, my dog Sultan, the holder of seventeen first prizes. This dog, a handsome boar-hound, standing about thirty-four inches high at the shoulders and weighing some two hundred pounds, had been presented to me as a puppy by Prince Bismarck. Though I have never specially trained him, the dog has remarkable intelligence. My companion throughout my tour in America, he used to jump into the luggage van at every journey's end to find my trunks, and those that were not too heavy for him to lift, he would bring out of the van. A similar performance would be repeated when we reached the hotel. Sultan would himself carry a good deal of the luggage upstairs, taking it up piece by piece, and disdaining the assistance of the niggers who would sometimes offer to give him help. Not unnaturally, he became a great favourite wherever we went, and, though it was against the regulations, the hotel managers would allow us to have him in our rooms. He would never go out without carrying a satchel containing his chain and muzzle, a box of pills, two brushes, a tooth brush, a comb, and a few pieces of flannel, which were used for rubbing him down and keeping his coat in careful condition. He seemed to know perfectly each of these contents, and if one was ever missing he would not be satisfied until it was found or replaced.

Sultan can carry me very easily. Once in America I sprained my foot. I happened to be staying at the time at about the only hotel in the country which is not furnished with elevators. My rooms were on the second floor, and that faithful and devoted creature would carry me up and down stairs before and after each performance, for I was still able to fulfil my engagements despite the sprain.

It is a peculiar thing about Sultan that, though he will not hurt you, yet if you enter a room whilst he is in it alone he will never let you leave until someone has attended to you. As a thief catcher, he is, for this reason, unequalled. On one occasion, as you shall hear, during my American tour, he saved my watch—that watch which was presented to me by my friend the French count. Whilst I am at the theatre I usually leave my coat and vest hanging on the wall of my dressing-room, Sultan being left in charge. One night we missed for more than an hour one of the stage assistants When I returned to my dressing-room I was unable for the moment to enter. Sultan, it appeared, was blocking the door. Pushing it open I found the missing assistant at the other end of the room in a state of some uneasiness. I asked him what he was doing, and he explained that he had come to see if he could offer me any assistance. Having entered the room, the dog would not let him move, and altogether he made out such a piteous tale that I sent him off with half-a-dollar. When, however, I came to look at my things I found that my watch, instead of being where I left it, in my vest pocket, was lying on the table, together with some money which had been taken from my pockets. It was then clear that the man's real object in entering my room was not that of assistance, but of robbery. I called him back, verified my suspicions, and had him immediately discharged. For that night's work we treated Sultan to a special steak for his supper.

This unfortunately was not the only adventure which I had with this watch of which I was so proud. My friend's gift seemed to be doomed. Whilst we were at Omaha there was a ball given in the city, and Mrs. Sandow and I were invited to be present. As we should be late in returning I told my valet to give Sultan his walk and then to take the dog home with him for the night. We reached home about half-past two in the morning, and being tired we went straight to bed. It may be explained that our bedroom stood behind the drawing-room, from which it was entered. Beyond the bedroom was the bathroom, in which I hung my clothes, leaving my watch and chain in my vest pocket.

I felt that night, as I felt on the " Elbe," that something was going to happen. Owing to this feeling I took the precaution to lock the drawing-room door. No one could enter the bedroom without coming through the drawing-room first. We felt, therefore, reasonably secure. In addition to my watch and chain, there was Mrs. Sandow's jewellery, which she had worn at the ball, whilst, amongst other special things, I had five twenty dollar pieces, which I had bought because of their rare dates. These gold pieces I left in my clothes in the bathroom ; Mrs. Sandow's jewellery remained in a drawer in the bedroom.

Through the night we slept without disturbance. In the morning the servant who came to look after our clothes noticed that my watch chain had been broken and that my watch was missing. The five twenty dollar pieces were also gone, but Mrs. Sandow's jewellery was untouched.

Questioned as to how she got into the room, the girl said that the door was open. Someone had evidently broken into our rooms whilst we slept and had worked so quietly that they had not disturbed us.

A detective was called, and it was ascertained that shortly after we returned from the ball two well dressed men entered the hotel and asked for rooms on the first floor. It was then between two and three o'clock. Before five o'clock they left. The detective remarked that about that hour two men answering the description that was given had been seen to enter a train, and he thought he would be able to succeed in tracing them. I told him that if he brought my watch back he should be well rewarded.

When the rooms were examined it was found that the door had been opened by means of an instrument which was pushed through the keyhole to turn the key. The gas had been half turned on during the night, and no doubt they saw my watch-chain shining in the uncertain light, and decided to take those things that they could lay their hands on most easily without fear of waking us. It might have been supposed to be risky work to rob a strong man ; but, on the other hand, it was found afterwards that the burglar was a desperate fellow, who had just completed nineteen years' penal servitude for shooting a man who was unfortunate enough to wake up whilst he was rifling his room.

During the day the two men were arrested. Four of the twenty-dollar pieces were found on them, but the watch was still missing. The men were taken before the police authorities, but on the ground that the case was not fully proved they were dismissed. After this decision, the detective came to me to ask what the watch was worth. Five hundred pounds I told him, in actual money, but for me it had a priceless value, and not for five thousand pounds would I willingly part with it.

" Seeing that it is worth so much," he said, " I will try to get it for you if you will promise to give me £800."

At this moment I realised the situation ; at any rate I felt justified in believing that this so-called detective was in league with the burglars, who had themselves owned in court that they knew where the watch was, though they refused flatly to give the information. Feeling disgusted with a man who could thus play so false and mean a game I took him by his neck and trousers and sent him flying through the door.

From that day to this I have never seen anything of my watch. It is, no doubt, lost to me for ever. If I had had my dog with me that night it would never have been stolen, for no burglar would have got past Sultan, however clever he might be at picking locks.

*   *   *   *

Throughout my tour I offered medals to those of my pupils who were able to show the highest developments under my system of physical training. Thousands of applications were received, and the amount of my correspondence was enormous. In the end I arranged a meeting, at which the pupils stripped for my personal examination, and there the awards were made.

I received also several challenges during my tour. These challenges were frequently made after I had left a city, and as it came to be clear that those who made them merely sought advertisement by associating their names with mine, I deposited ten thousand dollars with the "New York Herald" on the understanding that anyone who seriously meant business should also make a deposit as a guarantee of his good faith. If he duplicated my feats of strength the money would be his. But though this sum was deposited for about nine months I never received an answer. No one ever attempted to win that ten thousand dollars and I have the original cheque, made out to James Gordon-Bennett, to this day. I have had it framed and preserve it as a memento.

At the end of my first tour in America I returned to England, engaged fresh talent for my company, and invented and practised some new feats of strength, including that which I have entitled the Roman horse exercise, and that in which two people drive over me with a horse and chariot. Afterwards I paid a short return visit to America, to fulfil certain engagements, and then came back again to London.

———>·◄———

CHAPTER XII.

MY PERFORMANCE AT THE PRESENT TIME.

It may be useful, as a record, to indicate briefly the nature of the salient features of my recent performance at the London Pavilion, and since in the provinces.

To begin with there is a tableau, arranged for the purpose of showing muscular repose, with all the muscles relaxed; muscular tension, with all the muscles as firm as steel; the abdominal muscles; the biceps, muscles of the inside of the upper arm; the triceps, muscles of the back of the upper arm; the deltoid, muscles of the shoulders; the trapezius muscle, which raises the shoulders; the muscles of the back; the action and uses of different muscles; and the chest expansion, from 48ins. normal to 62ins.

The tableau curtains are drawn, and the scene changes to the arena. Resting with my neck on one trestle and my heels on another, I hold a 56lb. weight in each hand at arms' length and support four men simultaneously on my body. For the performance of this feat it may be mentioned that exceptionally strong neck and abdominal muscles are necessary.

Taking a pack of ordinary playing cards I tear them first in half, then in four parts, and finally into eighths. Next I tear two packs, and finally three packs, each pack containing the ordinary number of fifty-two cards. The feat of tearing in half one pack of cards was originally shown to me by the late Emperor of Russia. My reputation as an amateur had reached his Imperial Majesty, who paid me the honour of commanding my presence. During that interview his Majesty, as a test of his own manual strength, took a pack of cards and tore it, as I have said, in halves. He had never tried more than the one pack, but as is apparent I have succeeded with three, the torn cards being distributed each evening amongst the audience.

Another feat is performed lying prone on the ground. From this position I lift with one hand a Roman chariot, rising upright with it and afterwards lying down again. This feat brings the whole of the muscles into play.

I also introduce my Roman horse exercise. Sitting on a horse and so bending my back as to throw my head over the animal's tail I raise at arms' length heavy weights from the ground. Next I pick up two men, one after the other, raising them over my head and seating them in the saddle.

Another interesting feat consists of lifting a man from a prone position on the ground to the horse's back, using one hand only.

As a concluding feat, I support on my chest a bridge weighing 800 lbs. Over this bridge two persons drive a horse and chariot, making a total weight of about 3,200 lbs.

Sometimes, however, I conclude my performance by lifting with one hand at arm's length a platform upon which rests an ordinary piano, with a man seated playing upon it. Having lifted it, I march off the stage with the lot, the musician playing a lively tune as we go.

I have not attempted to enumerate all my feats here ; of course my performance has been varied from time to time. But a number of other feats have been referred to in the body of the book.

It may be interesting, perhaps, to add that I have recently composed a musical march, entitled "Marche des Athlètes," as well as a waltz, "Sandowia" and other pieces, which musicians have been kind enough to commend for their brightness and originality.

CHAPTER XIII.

MY MEASUREMENTS.

As a supplement to the previous chapter it may be stated here, in answer to many inquiries, that my own measurements, etc., at the present time are as set forth below. The first edition of the book was written rather hurriedly, and consequently one or two trifling inaccuracies crept in. These are now corrected :—

Age ...	...	...	...	32 years.
Weight	...	...	...	14 stone 6lbs.
Height	...	...	...	5 feet 9¼ inches.
Neck ...	...	...	...	18 inches.
Chest ...	...	...	...	48 ,,
Chest expanded	...	...	62 ,,
Waist	...	...	...	30 ,,
Hips ...	...	...	...	42 ,,
Thigh	..	...	...	26 ,,
Knee ...	...	...	..	14 ,,
Calf ...	...	...	...	18 ,,
Ankle	...	...	...	8½ ,,
Upper arm ...	...	...	19½ ,,
Forearm	...	...	...	16½ ,,
Wrist ...	...	...	...	7½ ,,

My strength, it may be added, is steadily increasing. If some one had told me two years ago that I should be able to perform the feats of strength that I now accomplish I would not have believed it. I feel sure, moreover, that in the natural course of things, my strength will continue to increase. With careful training the bodily strength ought to increase steadily until the forty-fifth year is reached.

The above appeared in the first edition. Pupils will be glad to hear that my belief has been fully justified, and that even since the book was first published, some eighteen months ago, there has been a very material increase in my strength.

THE THEORY
OF
PHYSICAL EDUCATION
IN
ELEMENTARY SCHOOLS.
BY
THOMAS CHESTERTON,
Organizing Teacher of Physical Education to the London School Board.
LATE CHIEF INSTRUCTOR AT THE ALDERSHOT GYMNASIUM.

Revised Edition now Ready : **THREE SHILLINGS.**

MANUAL OF DRILL
AND
PHYSICAL EXERCISES,
WITH OR WITHOUT DUMB-BELLS OR MUSIC.

For the use of Teachers and Instructors of Physical Exercises, Students in Training Colleges, &c , as taught in the London and other Board Schools, all Army Schools, Principal Public Schools, Civil Gymnasia, Polytechnic Institutions, and Evening Classes throughout the Country.

COMPILED AND ARRANGED FROM THE BEST AUTHORITIES BY

THOMAS CHESTERTON.

ILLUSTRATED FROM PHOTOGRAPHS.

Revised Edition : **THREE SHILLINGS.**

These works have been adopted by the London School Board, for use in their Schools; and also by the Director-General of Military Education, for use in all Army Schools.

THE MANUAL OF DRILL
AND
WAND EXERCISES
(WITH OR WITHOUT MUSIC).

For use in Elementary and Secondary Schools, Evening Continuation School Gymnastic Classes, Boys' Brigades, etc.

BY

THOMAS CHESTERTON.

PROFUSELY ILLUSTRATED.   ONE SHILLING

LONDON : GALE & POLDEN, LTD.,
2, AMEN CORNER, PATERNOSTER ROW, E.C.

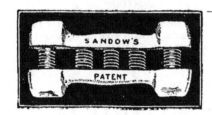

MY "GRIP" DUMB-BELL.

THE ordinary Dumb-bell, though excellent in itself, has one great defect, which I have been conscious of for years. In prescribing exercises for my pupils I am compelled to trust entirely to them as to the amount of will-power used whilst exercising. They may work energetically or slovenly according to their condition, but how they work is beyond my knowledge or control.

How to combat this has long engaged my attention, and after long years of study and experiment I have at last discovered a Dumb-bell which absolutely compels the pupil to throw the necessary amount of will-power into his work.

This appliance is very simple, and cannot go out of order. It consists of a Dumb-bell made in two halves, separated about 1½ inches from one another, the intervening space being occupied by small steel springs, which may be of any strength.

When exercising, the springs are compressed by gripping the Bells, and bringing the two halves close together, in which position they are kept until the exercise is over.

The pupil who possesses these Bells will find that instead of having to be continually buying heavier Dumb-bells, one pair will suffice him for all time. All that it will be necessary for him to do will be to purchase, at a small expense, new springs from time to time. All pupils are advised to use the "Grip" Dumb-bell upon the merits of which I need not enlarge.

I have always taught that muscle is developed by will-power, not by mechanical movement, and the simple principle of this latest invention is, by calling forth a continual exercise of will-power to obtain results impossible with any previous Dumb-bell.

Yours faithfully,

Eugen Sandow

SANDOW'S SCHOOLS OF PHYSICAL CULTURE.

Central Offices—**Sandow Hall, Savoy Corner, Victoria Embankment, W.C.**

LONDON ESTABLISHMENTS :

32, St. James's Street, London, S.W.—Chief West End School   At this School each pupil receives individual instruction. **Three Months' Course, £10 10s.**

115a, Ebury Street, London, S.W., close to Victoria Station, accessible from all parts. SANDOW's popular School at popular prices.   Classes for ladies and gentlemen, **Three Months' Course, £3 10s.**

Brook House, Walbrook, London, E.C., adjoining Mansion House. Bank and Stock Exchange. This School has been specially built for City men. Fitted with marble plunge bath, &c. **Three Months' Course, £10 10s.**

185, Tottenham Court Road, London, W. SANDOW's Residential School.   Forty bedrooms, restaurant, smoke-room, and two large airy gymnasia, 70 feet long, luxuriously fitted throughout. The prices at this school are within the reach of everyone. Bedroom from 10s. per week **Non=Residential Terms, Three Months' Course, £2 10s.**

Crystal Palace School, Sydenham.   Separate schools for ladies and gentlemen.

PROVINCIAL ESTABLISHMENT :

Oxford Street, Manchester. Classes for ladies and gentlemen.   **Three Months' Course, £5 5s.**

Inspection invited at all Schools.   Visitors will be shown over, and the system explained.

In addition to Mr. SANDOW's System of Physical Culture, boxing and fencing taught at all schools.

Prospectuses of any School sent on application.

Measurement Form for Postal Instruction.

See Figure on page 39.   Date............................

Name ....

Address ....

Heart...	Nature of Illness, if any...
Lungs	How long ago ?...
Digestion...	Physical Peculiarity, if any...
Age...	Medical Examination...
Occupation	Result...

Neck.	Chest contract'd.	Chest expanded.	Upper right arm.	Upper left arm.	Forearm right.	Forearm left.	Waist.

Thigh Right	Thigh Left.	Calf Right.	Calf Left.	Height.	Weight.	Measur'd by

Fill up this form correctly in black ink, and forward, together with Postal Order for **2/6,** to **EUGEN SANDOW, Sandow Hall, Savoy Corner, Victoria Embankment, W.C.**—Mark Envelope "*Instruction.*"

Sandow's Large Dumb-bell Chart given FREE with each First Course usual price 1/-